UNDERSTANDING END-TIME BIBLE PASSAGES

And putting Biblical Prophetic Events In Chronological order

By
R. A. Abell

Copyright © 2017 by Randy Abell
Allrights reserved

ISBN # 978-1-387-67695-8

An Initial Challenge

There are several benefits to studying prophecy for the believer, including a sense of security regardless of the state of world affairs. The more a Christian becomes aware of how things continually fit into God's plan, the more assurance the believer can have that God has everything under control, even when it seems like the world is out of control.

For this reason and more, many would like to learn what the Bible says about prophecy and the end times. Prophecy is interesting, to say the least, and the more someone learns about prophetic passages and topics, the more they enjoy talking about it and studying it all the more. There are of course, challenges to studying prophecy, and if we are not careful, it is easy to not only misinterpret but also to bring incorrect preconceived notions to a specific passage, often trying to force prophetic passages into what we want them to be.

As a balance to this, since the Bible itself says that Scripture helps explain Scripture, we would be wise to place and harmonize prophetic passages with other passages in the Bible. That would lend a higher degree of certainty to each interpretation.

A few chapters of this book will cover some topics that anyone wanting to understand prophecy must learn before trying to interpret and place end time events. And then the remaining chapters will look at several major end time topics and dive deeper into the passage looking for clues, often comparing Scripture for insight.

And in most cases, the additional look and comparison of other end time passages will allow us to harmonize and even place the end time event chronologically, putting it before or after other end time events.

There are a couple of misunderstandings concerning prophetic studies. One is that the topic of prophecy being looked at is seemingly too complicated and we just assume that there are no conclusions that can ever be drawn, which is incorrect because even though we may not be able to come to a complete conclusion, there are always things to learn that may indeed help us unlock other prophetic passages. The study of prophecy is not for the impatient!

In my experience, persistency in finding even the smallest of truths in one area of prophecy ends up helping with another area.

The second misunderstanding can actually be dangerous and that is to casually and irresponsibly insert current events into a prophetic timeline and make assertions that they know that the Lord will return soon. While the Scriptures seem to teach that there is likely nothing standing in the way of the Lord starting the clock on the end times, too many have forced Biblical passages onto current events rather than allowing the Scriptures to fully explain itself.

The first misunderstanding, where they assume they can't learn prophecy leaves a believer uniformed about how precise God's plan is and thus leaves that believer uncertain and often too meek concerning spiritual things. And the second misunderstanding, where every headline is claimed to fulfill a Bible prophecy and that the Lord is coming back next week, just discredits the impetuous who connect dots that aren't there and over time they become the prophecy boy who cried wolf too many times.

The right place to be is in between these two extremes. We are told in 2 Thessalonians and other passages that God does allow us to figure out some things and that there are blessings for those that read about the end times. And at the same time, the Bible warns against going to far and assuming that you've figured out when the Lord is going to return, just as Old Testament prophets were warned against saying that they'd heard from the Lord when they hadn't.

As with all things, there are extremes but if we put ourselves where the Scriptures lead and learn what they say, that is a simply wonderful place to be! And I hope this book will not only help with your understanding of God's Word but give you great comfort and confidence in the Lord!

How I Developed a Love for the Study of Prophecy!

My interest in eschatology (study of last things) began in my twenties with the purchase of a Ryrie Study Bible. I was teaching a young adult Sunday school class and thought a series on prophecy would be good for me to teach and I knew they'd find it interesting. That Bible provided helpful resources for teaching, notes on geography, history, word meanings and more. It later became clear to me that Charles Ryrie was considered an expert in the area of eschatology (*escha* is Greek for '*last things*') in most evangelical circles. As Ryrie's study Bible proved useful, I purchased other books of his, including several on prophecy.

Reading those basic books on the end times made me thirst for more information and I found many friends at church who were also eager to discuss the last days. I remember with fondness talking through prophetic events guys from my home church like Al Eernisee, John Hutts, Dan Anderson and Eric Price. These chats after Sunday services at Grace Baptist Temple in Bloomington Indiana were so inspiring to me as a young man.

Those days were before the days of buying books on-line, and so any Christian book stores around provided places to search for another read. Finding *Charting the End Times* by Tim LaHaye felt like finding a goldmine of end time charts, until I found the *Charts of Dispensational Truth* by Clarence Larkin, which is so complicated and full of detail, and provided even more information, so much so that one could study it for years.

When I was called to preach in my mid-thirties, I uprooted my family to attend seminary which of course brought some challenges. One was the occasional feelings of being older than most other students and that I was automatically somehow behind. But one sheer joy was the classes dealing with prophecy.

The great privilege came to attend Baptist Bible Graduate School of Theology in Springfield, Missouri, where among other professors, Dr. Myron Houghton was an adjunct professor teaching eschatology, on loan from Faith Baptist Seminary in Iowa. It was a pleasant surprise to learn that Dr. Houghton had been a student of Dr. Ryrie when he was at Dallas Theological Seminary.

After graduating and moving to Iowa to start a church, I continued my education at the seminary in Iowa where Dr. Houghton taught, taking almost every class available. I had another great privilege of attending a pastor's conference in Jacksonville, Florida at First Baptist of Jacksonville, where none other than Charles Ryrie conducted a deep study in areas of prophetic passages. I attended every lecture and hung on every study, listening intently to every question he answered. And when Dr. Ryrie found out that I was a student of Myron Houghton, he spent extra time with me in the afternoons. What a privilege!

And so while slowly snailing along with my continuing education while pastoring, doing a class or two a year, I came to thoroughly enjoy eschatology. After completing my second Master degree in Iowa, I started my Phd program at Louisiana Baptist University and when I had to zero in on a topic, the choice was easy. Though it was a continual challenge to work further for a another degree while pastoring a growing church, the topic made it interesting to me.

I love how prophecy allows us to see the big picture and to know that God has things well in hand. And so I hope that you will enjoy what is contained in these pages and that they will not only give some further insight into the end times, but my prayer would be that God's Word might stir your heart to long for the coming of the Lord. Let us, as the Lord said, watch and pray!

Contents

Introduction	12
The Call to Study and Understand Prophecy	15
Challenges to Studying and Placing End-Time Passages	19
Benefits to Harmonizing Prophetic Passages	29
Some Assumptions Before Starting	35
The Last Days	38
The Gathering of Israel and the Jewish Temple	44
The Rapture of the Saints	51
The Judgment Seat of Christ	60
The Marriage Supper of the Lamb	69
The Four Horsemen	73
The Rise of the Antichrist	83
The 144,000	96
The Invasion of Gog and Magog	105
Israel Believes	119
The Abomination of Desolation	129
The Two Witnesses	135
The Campaign of Armageddon	140

The Lord's Return	149
The Nations Judged	155
The Great White Throne	157
Conclusion	163
Chronological Timeline Of End Time Events	165
Bibliography	168
About the Author	175

Illustrations

1. Tribulation Events Map	14
2. Map of Ottoman Empire from 1850	27
3. Billboard Predicting Return of Christ	33
4. Bible Timeline of End Time Major Events	36
5. Seven Stages of Church History	41
6. Pre-Tribulation Rapture Timeline	54
7. Tribulation Timeline	55
8. Judgment Seat of Christ	56
9. What Happens after the Rapture	67
10. What Happens at a Jewish Wedding	68
11. Marriage Supper of the Lamb	71
12. The Four Horsemen	72
13. Comparison of Judgments	73
14. Characteristics of the Antichrist	83
15. The Unholy Trinity	92
16. The 144,000	103
17. 1874 Map of Ezekiel's War	105
18. Antichrist Gog attacks Israel from the Middle East	106

19. Table of Nations	107
20. Descendants of Noah	108
21. Map of End-Time Nations	111
22. Christ Appearing to the Jews in Tribulation	126
23. The Abomination of Desolation	132
23. Two Witnesses	137
24. Armageddon War	141
25. Armageddon	145
26. Return of Christ	151
27. Judgment of Sheep and Goats	153

Tables

1. Jewish Population of Israel	47
2. When Will the Gog-Magog Battle Happen?	112

Chapter 1
Introduction

C.S. Lewis said "When the author walks on the stage the play is over. God is going to invade, all right - something so beautiful to some of us and so terrible to others that none of us will have any choice left? For this time it will be God without disguise. It will be too late then to choose your side."[1] What a divisive time the end times will be! Not only will God force a decision upon the earth, but when He brings about that decision there will no middle ground, no one will be neutral, no one will have not taken sides, no one will have not made their choice.

And there can be no greater division than between the saved and the unsaved. The Apostle John wrote "*And shall come forth they that have done good, unto the resurrection of life and they that have done evil, unto the resurrection of damnation*" (John 5:29). The Apostle Paul wrote "*To the one we are the savour of death unto death; and to the other the savour of life unto life…*" (2 Corinthians 2:16).

When some hear the word *prophecy* or *end times*, they often think of the last book of the Christian Scriptures, that being Revelation. But what they often miss, is that those that have believed and listened to the God of the Bible have always looked forward to prophecy about the last days and it can be found all throughout the Scriptures.

Jacob can be found *prophesying* to his sons at the end of his life in the first book of the Bible "*And Jacob called unto his sons, and said, Gather yourselves together, that I may tell you that which shall befall you in the last days*" (Genesis 49:1).

And the word *prophecy* is mentioned in the last chapter of the last book of the Bible "*And if any man shall take away from the words of the book of this prophecy…*" (Revelation 22:19). And so it should not come as a surprise that God's people have from the beginning and will to the end, look for the last days.

All throughout the ages of man, those who have believed in God have not only been a witness to their own generation, but endured the grief of living in a fallen world. Yes, they willingly

---

[1]. C.S. Lewis, *Mere Christianity* (San Francisco: Harper, 2009), 47.

know they also are sinners, but they have believed on God's grace and thus look forward, expectantly to the end, when God Himself will make all things right again.

So these pages will humbly attempt to show that the prophecy is not limited just to the last book of the Bible but has been a theme of the Scriptures from the beginning. And we will also then attempt to place some of the major prophetic passages in a suggested chronological timeline, showing that many prophetic passages have more in common than at first supposed.

An example would be the three passages below, where all three, in different time periods talk about what is not for today's readers to know. Yes, there is a line of what we will not figure out but that being said, that means we can understand everything up to that line. The point is that prophecy has been interesting to God's people all throughout the ages, as it should be.

DAN 12:8-10	MAT 24:36	ACTS 1:7
And I heard, but I understood not: then said I…what shall be the end of these things? And he said, Go thy way, Daniel: for the words are closed up and sealed till the time of the end. Many shall be purified, and made white, and tried… and none of the wicked shall understand; but the wise shall understand.	But of that day and hour knoweth no man, no, not the angels of heaven, but my Father only.	And he said unto them, It is not for you to know the times or the seasons, which the Father hath put in his own power.

And as will be seen, there are many passages that touch on prophecy and End Times events and with some effort we can place and harmonize them as they can offer great insight, not only in the depth of eschatology but in assisting teachers and students of the Bible with a greater understanding. Now this is not an easy task, as the very nature of prophetic passages lends themselves to word pictures, symbolic illustrations, and grand language, which if not studied carefully, are easy to misapply or wrongly place and often misinterpret.

Many beginning students of prophecy like to jump to the passages that interest them but the challenge is to lay some ground work first. In so doing, the reader will be able to all the more enjoy prophecy and be able to thoughtfully place it in a Bible timeline.

With that said, I hope and pray that maybe by the end of the book, perhaps the chart below will hopefully seem overly simplistic. And at the end of the book, there is a suggested timeline of end time events and yes, you could look at that now if you wanted.

Traditional Tribulation chart that at first seems complicated but as someone learns the Bible passages about prophecy will be easily understood.

Chapter 2
The Call to Study and Understand Prophecy

Why is prophecy important? Well, the Scriptures are laden with prophetic passages and to stay away from Biblical prophecy would be to ignore large sections of the Bible. John wrote *"Blessed is he that readeth and they that hear the words of this prophecy..."* (Revelation 1:3a). So would the conclusion not be that if it is beneficial and important to the Lord for believers to read the prophecies of Revelation? Then wouldn't that be the same and even more beneficial if believers would not only read Revelation but all the prophetic passages related to it, in order to have a deeper and even fuller understanding.

It is important to note that when most of the Bible was written, it was almost all prophecy. Yes, many prophecies have been fulfilled, like the multiplication of Abraham's descendents, the Israelites conquering Canaan, the return of a remnant to Jerusalem after the Babylonian captivity, the preaching of John the Baptist, the Virgin Birth of Christ, His ministry, crucifixion, and resurrection. So in a sense, students of Scripture are actually studying prophecy all the time, but much of it is past prophecy, ...fulfilled.

As stated earlier, studying prophecy can be difficult. It might be compared to an extremely difficult puzzle, where some pieces are easy to put together but there are others sections that are much harder to place and take a lot of meticulous effort to find where they go and how they fit. So it is with prophetic passages. But the effort is always worth it and here are a few reasons...

1) Studying Prophecy Authenticates the Bible

Bible prophecy gives the clearest indication that it is the verifiable Word of God. While the world searches through the writings of secular future tellers like Nostradamus, Edgar Cayce, or the predictions of Jeane Dixon or follows horoscopes or seek advice from psychics, they are only to eventually be disappointed! And most of the world, for some reason, ignore the most credible source of information on future events, the Bible.

Yet the fulfilled prophecies of the Christian Scriptures are backed by historical data, archaeological evidence, and the staggering mathematical improbability of their occurrence merely being the result of chance. No other source of historical knowledge can make the same claims, and for good reason. That is primarily because no other source is the inspired Word of God. *"We have also a more sure word of prophecy; whereunto ye do well that ye take heed, as unto a light that shineth in a dark place, until the day dawn, and the day star arise in your hearts: knowing this first, that no prophecy of the scripture is of any private interpretation. For the prophecy came not in old time by the will of man: but holy men of God spake as they were move by the Holy Ghost"* (2 Peter 1:19-21).

2) Studying Prophecy Encourages the Believer to Live for God

The dedicated student of Bible prophecy and all they teach or preach it to, will always live a holier or more pleasing life for the Lord than if they knew nothing of prophecy. That's because to know the facts about the return of Christ and both the judgments and rewards motivate or perhaps warn the listener to be prepared. Paul the Apostle wrote *"For the grace of God that bringeth salvation to all men, teaching us that, denying ungodliness and worldly lust, we should live soberly, righteously, and godly in this present world; Looking for that blessed hope, and the glorious appearing of the great God and our Saviour Jesus Christ"* (Titus 2:11-13). Notice that the motivation that Paul speaks of is the *"appearing of...Christ"*!

Studying prophesy will bring the believer into contact with passages about not only the return of Christ, but the judgment of the wicked, the casting of the unsaved into hell, and how those who are faithful to Christ will be rewarded and justice brought to all things. Though the entire Bible is given for believers' instruction and edification and there are, of course, other great topics besides prophecy. But prophecy alone gives the student of it such motivation for living for God, that to remove it from the line-up, will leave him or her unprepared as the Lord said to *"Watch"*.

3) Studying Prophecy Promotes Sound Doctrine

Learning about God's plan from start to finish, as revealed in the Scriptures, gives the believer a sort of immunity to cults and false religions, as they often play on the general populace's ignorance of future events and fill their heads with fantastic stories.

Just as the people of Berea, who were known for *"searching the Scriptures"* (Acts 17:11), believers are encouraged to personally examine what people or religious leaders say and then study and compare that to what the Word of God says. So whether it is the Jehovah Witnesses or Mormons, Scientology or the Branch Davidians, or Harold Camping, who as a religious radio minister, claimed the Lord would return on May 11 of 2011, when believers know how God says the end times will come about and what will happen, they can dismiss those who have erred because these false teachers do not measure up by the yardstick of the Scriptures.[2] The best antidote to religious fanaticism and heretical sensationalism is an understanding of Bible prophecy.

4) Knowing Prophecy Helps with Evangelism

A verse that should strike readers of the book of Revelation is when John said he saw an angel *"And I fell at his feet to worship him. And he said unto me, See thou do it not: I am thy fellowservant and of thy brethren that have the testimony of Jesus: worship God for the testimony of Jesus is the spirit of prophecy"* (Revelation 19:10). Notice that the angel said that the *"spirit of prophecy"* is a testimony or witnesses of Christ! Prophecy not only shows that Jesus was the Messiah at His first coming but is a constant witness that Christ is the King of Kings and will come again.

As a believer learns more about prophecy, they will be able to witness more effectively. Since Christ is the theme of the

---

[2]. R. C. Sproul, Jr., "Harold Camping: False Prophet?," Ligonier Ministries, https://www.ligonier.org/blog/harold-camping-false-prophet/ (accessed December 1, 2017).

Bible and the center of the Gospel, knowing more about all the prophecies that spoke of His first coming provides proof to share and knowing prophecies pertaining to His second coming, just makes the Gospel even more pertinent and interesting.

Dr. Randy Lewis said that when trying to evangelize those that know a little concerning the Bible, whether they are Jewish or from a Church background, that the topic of prophecy can be helpful. He suggest posing questions that allow them to learn prophecy as it is like putting together a puzzle.[3]

5) Studying Prophecy Obeys What Jesus Said to Do

Of course Jesus wants His followers to know God's Word. And as an example to them, Jesus answered most questions with a quote from the Scriptures. But Jesus went even further when He rebuked the Pharisees for not knowing the Scriptures about prophecy. Listen to what Jesus said to them, *"The Pharisees also with the Sadducees came and tempting him that he would shew them a sign from heaven. He answered and said unto them, When it is evening, ye say, it will be fair weather: for the sky is red. And in the morning, it will be foul weather today: for the sky is red and lowring, O ye hypocrites, ye can discern the face of the sky, but can ye discern the signs of the times?"* (Matthew 16:1-3).

So if Jesus expected the spiritual leaders of His day to know prophecy and thus recognize the signs of His first coming, should not the expectation be the same for believers today and for them to be held to the same accountability. Yes, working through decisions concerning the interpretation of prophetic passages can be difficult but the Apostle Peter said that prophecy is *"a light that shineth in a dark place"* (1 Peter 1:19). So studying prophecy is worth the time and the effort!

---

[3]. Randy Lewis, "What Do You Say to Your Jewish Friends about Jesus?," C. S. Lewis Institute, http://www.cslewisinstitute.org/What_Do_You_Say_to_Your_Jewish_Friends_about_Jesus_page1 (accessed December 21, 2017).

Chapter 3
Challenges to Studying Prophecy and Placing End-Time Passages

One truth that a student of prophecy must grasp right off the bat is that though God knows everything that is going to happen, believers will only be able to know so much. Isaiah wrote of God "*Declaring the end from the beginning, and from ancient times the things that are not yet done, saying, My counsel shall stand and I will do all my pleasure*" (Isaiah 46:10). And when Jesus spoke of what believers will know concerning His second coming He said "*But of that day and hour knoweth no man, no not the angels of heaven, but my Father only*" (Matthew 24:36). So evidently there are some things that regardless of how much believers study, God has set limits on how much is going to be revealed.

But that should not keep believers from wanting to learn all that God allows! The Apostle Paul, when writing to the believers in Thessalonica, who were what some call 'Prophecy Hounds', as they always had lots of questions about future events, wrote "*But of the times and the seasons, brethren, ye have no need that I write unto you. For yourselves know perfectly that the day of the Lord so cometh as a thief in the night*" (1 Thessalonians 5:1-2).

And when Paul uses the phrase "*times and seasons*", he is not talking about what day it is on the calendar or whether it is spring or fall, but referring to the things that will foretell the coming of prophetic events. As already mentioned, Jesus used the practice of looking at the sky to discern the weather as an illustration of how His followers should be looking for signs of prophetic events. And in another passage, Jesus told His disciples "*Now learn a parable of the fig tree: When his branch is yet tender and putteth forth leaves, ye know that summer is nigh: So likewise ye, when ye shall see all these things, know that it is near, even at the doors*" (Matthew 24:32-33). The Lord certainly encourages His followers to study prophecy!

But there will be some challenges. Prophetic studies are not the easiest but it seems that God in His wisdom has His reasons for that. Perhaps the Lord thinks it is best that brand new

Christians need some doctrinal teachings and if prophecy was easy, they might jump right into it before they were ready. Perhaps, God wanted to allow studying prophecy to be challenging because some find it a real challenge and enjoy that. Where the deeper they dig, the more precious the truth that is found! Regardless, there are some challenges to studying and especially harmonizing and placing end time prophetic passages in the Bible and here are some things to consider.

1) Prophecy Must Be Studied Through a Correct Doctrinal Prism

Now that may at first go against the grain of those who sincerely want to study prophecy and let the Scriptures speak for themselves but consider this example. If a scientist does research in their area of study, they do not just start experimenting but set up their experiments so that under certain conditions, they will find what happens. Now that does not mean they are not constantly evaluating whether the conditions or prism they are looking at the experiments through needs adjusted, but facts by themselves are not organized and often have to have a grid or a template. In the case of prophecy, a timeline or doctrinal position to place them in as they are studied is not determining what is found but allows the prophecy student to see if the many prophetic Bible passages fit in the prism or conditions that they are looking at them through.

For example, we will look at prophecy from a view that is dispensational, which means we know that Ephesians 3:2 means there are different ages of God dealing with people when it speaks of "*...the dispensation of the grace...*". So Moses lived in the era under the law and Paul lived in the age of grace. We'll also look at prophetic passages with a pre-millennial view and will apply a literal method of interpretation, which Tim LaHaye says is the grammatical-historical approach to Scriptures.[4] Chapter 4 will talk much more about this.

---

[4]. Tim LaHaye and Thomas Ice, eds., *The End Times Controversy: The Second Coming Under Attack* (Eugene, OR: Harvest House, 2003), 71.

2) Prophecies Sometimes Speak of Future Events As If They Were Present

An example of this would be a verse predicting the birth and later reign of Christ *"For unto us a son is given: and the government shall be upon his shoulder and his name shall be called Wonderful, Counselor, The Mighty God, The Everlasting Father, The Prince of Peace. Of the increase of His government and peace there shall be no end, upon the throne of David, and upon His kingdom, to order it, and to establish it with judgment and with justice from henceforth even for ever…"* (Isaiah 9:6-7).

In these two verses there are actually several tenses. Isaiah states that a son *"is given"*, clearly present tense, even though it would be hundreds of years before the birth of Christ. And in the same prophecy, Isaiah gives a reference to the past by basing this prophecy as almost starting with the *"throne of David"*, but looks to the future by stating that the government *"shall be upon His shoulder"* and His name *"shall be…"*.

Sometimes the reader does not catch all of a prophecy, especially when they may not be looking for one while just reading through the Old Testament. That is sometimes because the writer uses the present tense, like in the book of Isaiah, but it is obvious that the thought is actually from God Himself who has the miraculous ability to weave past, present and future all together because God is able to see time as a whole. From God's perspective, there doesn't even have to be past, present or future.

When John the Evangelist wrote the book of Revelation, he was writing in the here and now, although what he wrote about would not happen for thousands of years. But John was seeing future events sometimes as if they'd already happened.

John used the phrase *"I saw"* twenty eight times, twenty six of them from chapter four on, which as will be discussed, are future events. An example is *"And after these things, I saw four angels standing on the four corners of the earth…"* (Revelation 7:1). In this verse, John writes as if some events have transpired *"after these things"* and seems aware of time but then sees the future *"I saw"* as if in the present.

3) Sometimes Prophecy Can Portray the Future As If It Has Already Happened

As just mentioned in the writings of John in Revelation, when God allows a prophet to see the future, some of what he sees may seem as if it has already happened. J. Dwight Pentecost speaks of this and uses Isaiah 53 as an example of what he calls the time element, in this case, speaking of future prophecies as if they have already happened.[5] In Isaiah 53, which is of course, a detailed prophecy about the Lord's arrest and beatings and crucifixion, Isaiah speaks of it in past tense. Verse three says "*He <u>was despised</u> and we esteemed Him not…*". Verse four says "*He <u>hath borne</u> our greifs …*". Verse five says "*He <u>was wounded</u> for our transgressions…*".

There are at least nineteen past tense verbs in the chapter, which are all actually future events and at the same time at least fourteen future tense verbs in the same chapter, and sometimes both past and future tense verbs are in the same verse. Notice the past tense "*pleased*" and the future tense "*shall*" in the following "*Yet it pleased the Lord to bruise Him; he hath put him to grief: when thou shalt make his soul an offering for sin, he shall see his seed, he shall prolong his days, and the pleasure of the Lord shall prosper in his hand*" (Isaiah 53:10).

Believers need to understand that when these prophets saw the future, that they often described it as past or present. And as pointed out, only shows that the passage is inspired by God who sees past, present and future all at the same time.

4) Some Prophecies Contain a Double Reference

A double reference prophecy will contain a prophecy that could be looked at as already fulfilled but at the same time, contain a prophecy that has yet to be fulfilled.

These are simply amazing, as they show just how smart God is. And the coolest thing that the reader can notice is that as they are read, it is as if it is talking about the same event but on

---

[5]. J. Dwight Pentecost, *Things to Come: A Study in Biblical Eschatology* (Findlay, OH: Dunham, 1958), 46.

further study, it becomes clear that God had intended the passage to refer to something near and something far at the same time. J. Dwight Pentecost who takes considerable time in writing about this in depth defines a double reference as "two events, widely separated as to the time of their fulfillment, may be brought together into the scope of one prophecy".[6]

This was done because the particular prophet not only had something to say to the people of his time and the events of his day but it is clear that God had evidently given and woven into that prophecy a message about the far away future. There are many double reference prophecies, including one from Isaiah where the prophet gives a prophecy of his own child and at the same time, prophesying of a virgin born Messiah (Isaiah 7:14).

There is also the passage when the prophet Joel who wrote of God's pouring His Spirit out (Joel 2:28-30), and it was partially fulfilled in Acts 2, and yet still waiting for the end times to see "*I will shew wonders in the heaven and in the earth, blood, and fire, and pillars of smoke*" (Joel 2:30). But perhaps the most complex is found in Daniel, chapter eleven and the prophecies that speak of Antiochus IV, who was the Greek/Seleucid general of Syria during the time of the Maccabees, while at the same time describing many details concerning the Antichrist that will come many years later in the book of Revelation.[7]

A quick look at Daniel eleven has clear references to Antiochus "*He shall also set his face to enter with the strength of his whole kingdom, and the upright ones with him; thus shall he do: and he shall give him the daughter of women, corrupting her: but she shall not stand on his side, neither be for him*" (Daniel 11:17). This verse fits Antiochus perfectly, as the Seleucid king gave his daughter, Cleopatra, to marry the seven year old Ptolemy in 192 BC but this diplomatic marriage failed because Cleopatra sided with her husband against her father.[8] And then

---

[6]. Pentecost, 46.

[7]. Dennis McCallum and Gary DeLashmutt, "Double Reference in Biblical Prophecy," Xenos Christian Fellowship, https://www.xenos.org/essays/double-reference-biblical-prophecy (accessed February 23, 2016).

[8]. Flavius Josephus, *Josephus: Thrones of Blood*, ed. Toni Sortor (Uhrichsville, OH: Barbour, 1988), 17.

chapter 11:21-35 describes the rise and activities of Antiochus IV.

But as the chapter continues, it comes to a transitional statement "*And some of them of understanding shall fall, to try them and to purge and to make them white, even to the time of the end: because it is yet for a time appointed*" (Daniel 11:35). Notice the verse mentions "*understanding*" and then shifts to "*the time of the end*". And from then on through the rest of the chapter, even though it is still talking about a 'king', he is not Antiochus but none other than the Antichrist, as most of the details listed do not fit Antiochus but someone who comes along later in history. The most obvious is when it says "*And at the time of the end shall the king of the south push at him and the king of the north shall come against him like a whirlwind…*" (Daniel 11:40). This cannot be describing Antiochus for he was the king of the north, as all directional reference what direction something or someone is from Israel.

So Daniel 11 is a great and complex example of how God used a passage to both prophecy of something in the near future, Antiochus IV, who would ravage Palestine before the days of Christ, while at the same time, prophecy of details of the Antichrist, who will ravage Palestine at some point in the future.

5) Sometimes Prophecies Are Conditional

Conditional prophecies can also throw the Bible student off if effort is not made to do their diligent work in a Bible study, basically to see what happened after a prophecy was given. The book of Jeremiah is filled with conditional prophecies and if the reader came across the early chapters of Jeremiah where God told Jeremiah to tell Israel that He was going to allow them to be wiped out forever, the reader would be remiss not to find that later in the same book, God further explained that the warning was conditional.

Furman Kearley says "The case for conditional prophecy must begin with the most explicit, the most extensive, and the most generic statement of the principle as found in Jeremiah 18:1-12".[9] It is in this passage that the Lord just plainly states that He has the right to make statements concerning nations about whether He will bless or chastise them, but that if they change their ways, He will "*repent*" or change what was going to happen to them. So though most prophecies concerning the End Times are not conditional, there are a few.

6) We Must Be Careful Not to Assume They Understand a Prophetic Passage Just Because They Have Been Taught a Certain Interpretation by Someone

Many students of prophecy can likely remember hearing a prophetic passage preached or taught with what seemed like a reasonable interpretation, only to have events undo that interpretation as the years rolled by. Roberts Mounce states that the word "*shortly*" in Revelation 22:6 is often misunderstood and that *imminence* is not the same as *immediate*. He points out that "John writes that these events which constitute the revelation must take place shortly or as we would understand the word to mean right away. That more than 1900 years of church history have passed and the end is not yet poses as a problem for some".[10] And that is because they have made wrong assumptions or not done a word study to verify a meaning of a phrase or verse.

So when Israel became an officially recognized nation in May of 1948, many preachers and evangelists started preaching that the Lord would return before 1988, which was based on their understanding of Matthew 24 and the Lord saying that He would return before a generation passed. They just knew that a generation was forty years and that the fig tree of Matthew 24 was blooming and put it together that they had a 'no later than' timeline for the Lord's return. Well, when 1988 came and went, obviously, that was a wrong interpretation. It was not that they were intentionally preaching false doctrine and trying to lead people astray, in fact, just the opposite, as they were trying to get people's attention and warn them that the Lord might return soon,

---

[9]. Furman Kearley, *The Conditional Nature of Prophecy* (Montgomery, AL: Apologetic Press, n.d.), 5.

[10]. Robert Mounce, *The Book of Revelation*, The New International Commentary on the New Testament (Grand Rapids: William Eerdmans, 1977), 64–66.

but the way they did it, ended up undermining their reputation when they were wrong.

Later, some reinterpreted the passage to mean that a generation was seventy years and so again in 2011, which was 2018 minus the seven years of Tribulation, others still wrongly predicted the return of Christ. And then in September of 2017, an alignment of planets sent another round of predictions about the return of Christ.[11]

Another example is the passage that talks about *"the one being taken and the other left behind"* (Matthew 24:40-41). Many have came across these verses and automatically assumed that this is referring to the Rapture, and most would agree that it sure preaches well. But when the entire passage is studied and put into context, these verses cannot be talking about the Rapture. When this has been preached incorrectly, the one taken is going to heaven and the one left is going into the Tribulation, but in fact, it is just the opposite. The one left gets to go into the Millennial Kingdom and the one taken is taken for judgment.

The correct view places the passage at the end of the Tribulation when Christ has returned to judge. Now not everyone agrees with that position, for instance John Phillips explains the passage as not being in chronological order but topical.[12] But the point would be that many will hear a sermon preached or a commentary written and just assume the interpretation is correct.

A third example would be the early church's assumptions that they knew who the Antichrist was. They at first thought it was the Roman Emperor Nero and many early Christian writings made those claims such as the *Sibylline Oracles*, which was a collection of Jewish and Christian apocalyptic verses that literally named the Roman Emperor as the fulfillment of the Antichrist.[13]

And later even such great theologians as Martin Luther

---

[11]. Daniel Matson, "The Great Sign of Revelation 12 Occurs in 2017," Signs of the End, http://watchfortheday.org/1260tetrad.html (accessed September 29th, 2017).

[12]. John Phillips, *Exploring the Gospel of Matthew*, John Phillips Commentary Series (Grand Rapids: Kregel, 1999), 460.

[13]. Edward Champlin, *Nero* (Cambridge, Massachusetts: Harvard University Press, 2003), 90–92.

thought that Pope Leo X was the Antichrist. And with how the Roman Catholic Church were persecuting anyone who looked to the Scriptures instead of to Rome, it is easy to understand how in Luther's day, the Pope seemed to be fulfilling the prophecies of who the Antichrist would be.

    A final example that is still unfolding is the interpretation of the Daniel passages regarding the Ten Nation Confederation and the giant statue that Nebuchadnezzar saw *"And the fourth kingdom shall be strong as iron…And whereas thou sawest iron mixed with miry clay, they shall mingle themselves…"* (Daniel 2).

    Throughout recent decades, the iron mixed with clay has been taught as a revived Roman Empire, John Phillips teaches this for example.[14] And when Phillips, along with many others saw the rise of the European Union they assumed this was the old Roman Empire taking shape to fulfill prophecy. But now that the European Union no longer has ten nations in league but currently 28, that no longer seems to fit. And a new theory is that the fourth empire of Daniel 2 was not the Roman but the old Ottoman empire.[15]

    Sometimes, a view has been taught so long with everyone just assuming it was correct, that even when history and events start to make it no longer fit the prophetic prism, inconsistencies are ignored only because believers don't adjust their thinking. If prophecy is to be taught correctly, the teacher should be a little more cautious before and not assume that past interpretations are correct. So will the European Union somehow in the future shrink to fit the Ten Nation Confederacy, just as Great Britain recently withdrew? Or will there be a Islamic Ten Nation Confederacy where the old Ottoman Empire once was? Or will there be some new confederation of nations from which the antichrist will rise? Only time or some new unlocked prophetic passage will tell.

---

[14]. John Phillips, *Exploring the Book of Daniel*, John Phillips Commentary Series (Grand Rapids: Kregel, 2004), 50.

[15]. Joel Richardson, *Mideast Beast: The Scriptural Case for an Islamic Antichrist* (Washington, D.C.: WND Books, 2012), 60.

Map of the Ottoman Empire in 1850, which is one consideration for the last empire of Daniel's vision. The other more traditional view is the old Roman empire. One interesting point for the Ottoman Empire view is that the Roman empire never really controlled Babylon, from which Daniel wrote but the Ottoman Empire did and some think that since it was Nebuchadnezzar's dream, that Babylon must have been controlled by the empires that he dreamed about.

Chapter 4
Benefits to Harmonizing Prophetic Passages

There are many benefits to studying and trying to harmonize prophetic passages as they bring spiritual wisdom and maturity to the believer. There are many aspects of this but here are at least four great reasons to study prophecy to the degree that Christians can have an understanding of it.

1) They Will Not Be Fooled

In Matthew 24-25, the Lord stresses several times to those listening to Him to pay attention to prophetic events. He tells his disciples that they are to "*…Take heed that no man deceive you*" (Matthew 24:4). And the Lord goes on in the next verse to say that there will actually be many that come in the name of Christ with all sorts of claims and that their arguments are persuasive enough that many follow them.

Jesus says later in the passage that there will be "*many false prophets*" and that they will "*deceive many*" (Matthew 24:11). This particular section of Scripture does not say but we can only imagine the many ways that mankind is deceived by all sorts of strains of apostasy and heresy. This is easily explained that though Satan is thrilled with the wickedness of the world, he is likely spending most of his time trying to destroy Christianity from within. John Goetsch says that "Satan rarely acts like Satan - He acts like God".[16] He disguises himself so that many "do not recognize that it is him" and it must be remembered that the Apostle Paul talked about that very thing when he wrote "*And no marvel; for Satan himself is transformed into an angel of light*" (2 Corinthians 11:14).

Later in Matthew 24, Jesus actually tells those in the last days that they should not believe those who say they know where Christ is and He says "*…believe it not*" (Matthew 24:23).

---

[16]. John Goetsch, *Contemporary Compromise: Standing for Truth in an Age of Deception* (Lancaster, CA: Striving Together, 2010), 73.

Jesus goes on and tells readers to "*Learn a parable of the fig tree…*" and that believers are to look for signs that "*summer is nigh*" (Matthew 24:32).

In Matthew 25, Jesus tells the parable of the wise and foolish virgins, showing that the wise had prepared and by application, had thought things through, while the foolish virgins had not prepared (Matthew 25:1-10). Yes, studying prophecy will keep believers from being fooled.

2) They Will Not Be Deceived

The Thessalonians were very interested in studying prophecy. Imagine where believers today would be without the completed New Testament. But that did not stop the Thessalonians, as they must have poured through the Old Testament, likely some early copies of the Gospels, and perhaps some of Paul's writings or maybe even some sermons that he had preached there. And they had some questions and by answering them, Paul makes a second point as to a benefit of knowing prophecy.

It seems that they had written him with some concerns that they did not want to miss the rapture and should they be trying to figure out who the Antichrist was.[17] To this Paul responds "*Now we beseech you by (about) the coming of our Lord Jesus Christ and by (about) our gathering unto him, that ye be not soon shaken…as that the day of Christ is at hand*" (2 Thessalonians 2:1-2).

So Paul was reminding them of the questions they had asked and goes on to say that they should "*Let no man deceive you…*" (2 Thessalonians 2:3) and then goes into detail concerning the Antichrist, telling them that true Christians will be removed before the Antichrist makes his appearance. But those who are not saved and do not know about the end times will be taken in by "*signs and lying wonders*" and "*deceivableness of unrighteousness*" (2 Thessalonians 2:9-10).

---

[17]. John Phillips, *Exploring 1 and 2 Thessalonians*, John Phillips Commentary Series (Grand Rapids: Kregel, 2005), 167.

In his detailed work on the Antichrist, A.W. Pink goes to great length to point out just how deceiving satan's man will be and for those without the Holy Spirit dwelling in them and no knowledge of the prophetic Scriptures that warn of him, that most of mankind will be taken in.[18]

3) They Will Not Be Impetuous

Imagine how many prophecy related questions the Apostle Paul was asked? As just noted, the Thessalonians were jumping to wrong conclusions by having the prophecy timeline far forward of where it actually was. And we could likely presume the Thessalonians were not the only ones. Today, the same problem can be observed, with some either setting dates for the Rapture or stating that believers today are already in the Tribulation or by misinterpreting prophetic passages to undo the imminency of the Lord's return.

One example of pushing the timeline farther forward would be Arnold Murray of Shepherds Chapel, who has not only predicted a date for the battle of Armageddon, which by the way, according to him, was thirty years ago at the writing of this book, but teaches openly that believers today are in the Tribulation time period. Of course, he has set a date for the Lord's return, and of course, the Lord did not return, which made him and his organization look like fools, which they were.[19]

And one only has to slightly explore the history of the Jehovah Witness movement or the Seventh Day Adventist movement to find out that they did much the same thing in not really placing and harmonizing prophetic passages which allowed them to take some out of order and wrongly predict the Second coming of Christ over and over again, of course incorrectly.[20]

So when the Apostle Paul wrote that believers need to be careful in judging things until the Lord comes *"Therefore judge*

---

[18]. Arthur W. Pink, *The Antichrist* (Blacksburg, VA: Wilder, 2008), 94.

[19]. "Arnold Murray: The Shepherd's Chapel," Let Us Reason Ministries, http://www.letusreason.org/poptea4.htm (accessed December 1, 2017).

[20]. Walter Martin, *The Kingdom of the Cults*, rev. ed., ed. Ravi Zacharias (Minneapolis: Bethany House, 2003), 53.

nothing before the time, until the Lord come…" (1 Corinthians 4:5), it is likely that he had those who made wrong assumptions in prophecy in mind.

In Bible believing circles, excitement about the coming of the Lord sometimes gets the best of Scriptural discernment, even though evangelical Christians make such an effort about applying Scriptures wisely. Even in fundamental circles, which seemingly tend to be stewards of protecting the truth against false teachers, there may not be date setters but the sensationalism often comes close. A common quip is that the Lord said believers would not know the day or the hour but the verse does not say anything about the year. That is dangerous thinking as even the famous evangelist Jack Van Impe came dangerously close to predicting 2012 as the year the Lord would return.[21] It was not that he was ignoring Scripture or trying to lead anyone astray, but was just so excited about what seemed to him as signs of the end times, that he could not help but surmise publically that it seemed the Lord might return soon.

Another case of sensationalism was when the year 2000 was approaching and all the talk concerning whether the Lord was going to return. Most of this was based on the young earth theory, where if one believes that the earth is just shy of 6,000 years old, some use the Creation account and say that God labored for six days and rested the seventh, so the earth will go 6,000 years laboring in sin and then 1,000 millennial reign of Christ. And so in the year 2,000, many well meaning Christians went out and bought generators and stocked up on canned goods and bottled water. Well, nice theory, as I tend to believe the young earth view, but those who knew prophetic passages knew that the moment that everyone predicted that was the day, meant that it was not the day. And if we think He may indeed return after 6,000 years, we should have checked the Jewish calendar which is around 150 years behind the Gregorian calendar. So on the Jewish calendar, it's still a few years to go.

---

[21]. Alan Torres, "Jack Van Impe: Bible Prophecy Teacher Extraordinaire or Confused Prophet?," The Biblicist, http://biblicist.chrisapproved.com/bible/vanimpe.html (accessed November 30, 2017).

The point is that by knowing more than just the famous prophetic passages and trying to fit them together, a balance of Scripture will keep believers from being impetuous and making wrong claims, specifically about the coming of Christ.

4) *They Will Not Be Late in Being Ready*

Though the Scriptures say that dates should not be set for the return of Christ, that does not mean that the followers of Christ should not be watching for the signs of the Lord's coming. There is a fine line between staying current on world events and always assuming they mean something prophetically. We should be considering how they might play out and possibly fit a prophetic prism, but at the same time, be careful in thinking that we have found or unlocked something that gives an individual or group some special insight into when the Lord is going to return. But that doesn't mean we shouldn't be watching.

The verse in Hebrews is intriguing when it says *"Not forsaking the assembling of ourselves together, as the manner of some is; but exhorting one another: and so much the more as ye see the day approaching"* (Hebrews 10:25). Notice the phrase *"as ye see the day approaching"* and how the author of Hebrews just assumes that those that are faithful to church and staying connected to the Scriptures will *"see the day approaching"*. How many times did the Lord say "Watch"! Watch what? He did not intend for believers to be staring at the sky every day, but watching, looking, taking heed, studying so that when the fig tree buds start to swell, when the sky is red in the evening, when the pieces of the puzzle start to come together and all the prophecy clocks are close to midnight, that the student of prophecy will just sort of know that His coming is close.

Paul so much as said that very thing to the Christians in Thessalonica when he said *"But of the times and the seasons, brethren, ye have no heed that I write unto you. For yourselves know perfectly that the day of the Lord so cometh as a thief in the night...But ye brethren, are not in darkness, that that day should overtake you as a thief"* (1 Thessalonians 5:2-4).

Here in one passage, believers are told that the Lord will on one hand come unannounced, as a thief in the night, but on the other hand, believers can look at the times and the seasons and be able to know if things are lining up. Paul told the Thessalonians that they were not in darkness, as they were saved and the Lord's coming will not be like a thief in the night to believers. The Pulpit commentary puts it well in saying that while Paul was clearly telling them that the timing of the Second Advent was beyond his knowledge to teach, that they themselves could keep watch.[22] How wise!

Besides all these reasons there are in harmonizing end time passages, there is also a benefit to being able to place many of them chronologically. They bring more understanding to the passage when we know that it, for example, is referring to the Tribulation and especially if it allows us to know when in the Tribulation it might take place.

Billboard wrongly predicting the return of Christ in 2011 by Herold Camping and Family Radio - It made him and all those that listened to him look like a fool. Even worse, the news media became even more desensitized to the real return of Christ.

---

[22]. H.D.M. Spence and Joseph S. Exell, *Pulpit Commentary* (Peabody, MA: Hendrickson, 2011), 21:103.

Chapter 5
Some Assumptions Before Starting

Before diving into the some prophetic topics, it is helpful to know certain terms and how we will be looking at the passages concerning the end times. In a way, we are sort of laying out a grid to help us interpret prophecy. This is in no way forcing the Scriptures into a belief system but only looking at them through a prism of conditions, just like a scientific researcher would.

First, we will approach the passages with a literal grammatical interpretation. And what does that mean? Being a literalist when it comes to interpretation does not mean there is not a spiritual meaning and it does not mean that the prophecy student would not recognize figurative language. Dwight Pentecost said "The Literalist is not one who denies that figurative language, that symbols, are used in prophecy, nor does he deny that great spiritual truths are set forth there: his position is, simply that the prophecies are to be normally interpreted…".[23] So unless the Scriptures tell us that something is symbolic or illustrative, we will assume the passage is to taken literally.

We will also look at prophecy in consideration of the many covenants that God made with believers throughout the ages. Of course there are thousands of promises from God but there are several that took the form of a contract, very formal, very specific, and very eternal, which is why they shape an understanding of prophecy.

The theologian Alva McClain list several covenants: The Abrahamic (sometimes called the Palestinian), the Mosaic, the Davidic, and the New Covenant (sometimes called the Covenant with the Church).[24] Though the covenants will not be covered in this book, their importance cannot be ignored and at least must be mentioned as part of the prism of how a student of prophecy should approach the Bible. Because God keeps His promises!

In general, they look at the descendants of Abraham as the recipients of the land known as Palestine and that the tribes of

---

[23]. Pentecost, 13.

[24]. Alva McClain, *The Greatness of the Kingdom: An Inductive Study of the Kingdom of God* (Winona Lake, IN: BMH Books, 2001), 33.

Israel that Moses led out of Egypt will one day receive the land grant of all of Palestine, even larger than Israel was during the reign of King Solomon. The <u>Davidic covenant</u> looks to a descendent of David to rule and reign on Israel's throne, from the pre-millennial perspective in the Millennial kingdom. And the <u>New Covenant</u> is that which is sometimes applied to Israel one day being revived again as the people of God, although some apply it to the church being the Bride of Christ, although both views actually do not contradict each other.

      Understanding all of these covenants usually brings someone to a place where they realize that the church has not replaced Israel because of the promises made specifically to Israel. And while the church holds a blessed place in God's plan, it is clear that God is not done with Israel and that after the church has been removed or taken to heaven, that God's plan for Israel will then start again. Sometimes this view is referred to as Dispensational theology.

      Author Tim LaHaye defines Dispensationalism as viewing "the world and history as a household run by God. In this household world, God is dispensing or administering affairs according to His own will and in various stages of revelation with the passage of time".[25] One could also say that dispensationalism just looks at how God has dealt with mankind. For instance, the Old Testament believer was asked to obey the Law given from Moses because that is all they had. But the New Testament believer is asked to know all the Scriptures and then obey Christ. And so with Dispensational Theology in mind, we can easily comprehend that the church will not bring in the Millennial kingdom but that the 1,000 year predicted kingdom of the end times is for Israel so that God can fulfill His promises to them.

      This view is called the Pre-millennial view, which places the return of Christ for the church <u>before</u> the Millennial kingdom. In addition to that, there is also a term for the view that Christ will return to call Christians home before the seven years of Tribulation. That view is called Pre-Tribulation, "pre" meaning 'before'.

---

[25]. Tim LaHaye and Thomas Ice, *Charting the End Times: A Visual Guide to Understanding Bible Prophecy* (Eugene, OR: Harvest House, 2001), 81.

So the Pre-Tribulational/Pre-Millennial view of prophecy looks at the church age as coming to an end with when Christ returns for the church to call us home to heaven, which then starts the seven years of Tribulation. This is sometimes called Jacob's Seventieth week. During the seven years of Tribulation God both calls Jews into belief in Christ and at the same time unleashes His wrath on the unbelieving earth. At the end of this period, the Bible says that Christ then returns to the earth for the One Thousand year Millennium. That period is primarily for the Jews although Christians will return with Christ to rule and reign with Him, evidently in the rest of the world that was not promised to Israel.

All that said, as we look at many prophetic passages of Scripture, we'll be looking at them through the Pre-tribulational, Pre-millennial view.[26]

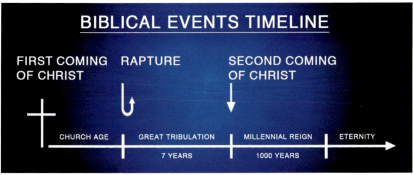

Here is a simplified view of when Christ returns for the Church, which then allows the seven years of Tribulation, followed by the Second coming of Christ and then the Millennium. This view is called the Pre-Trib/Pre-Millennial view.

---

[26]. Pentecost, 193.

Chapter 6
The Last Days

To start a look at prophecy, this being the first chapter that looks at a specific topic, there is nowhere else to start but to look at the time period that falls at the end of the church age, commonly known in evangelical circles as 'The Last Days'.

In the Gospel of Luke, the Lord Jesus asked *"when the Son of Man cometh, shall He find faith on the earth?"* (Luke 18:8). What a great question! And just as a history student would study the time leading up to a significant event to understand what led to it, a student of prophecy really has to begin with the days leading up to the great events of the end times. In the view point of those who hold a pre-tribulation, pre-millennial rapture, those saved in the church age will not be here on earth for the seven years of tribulation, but they will be here for the last days. So just as much thought and study should be given to the last days that believers should be watching and living in and not just the end of those days that believers are watching for.

The phrase "last days" is used in differing degrees in Scripture referring to the *End times* seven times, although there are of course, more ways to say it, like *"Day of the Lord"*, that "Great Day" and many others. But two very distinct and precise passages that describe the days leading toward the return of Christ actually use the phrase "last days" and are 2 Timothy 3 and 2 Peter 3. We will compare those passages and try to place them in the book of Revelation timeline.

Both of these books were written within a few years of each other. Peter's second epistle was written near the end of his life between 63-65A.D., as most scholars place his death no later than 68A.D.[27] And Paul had to have written his second letter to Timothy around 66A.D. as Paul was martyred, according to Eusebius, in 67A.D..[28] With that in mind, both of these Apostles were aware of the same things going on in the church, some good and some not. And the Holy Spirit laid on each of their hearts

---

[27]. D. A. Caron, Douglas J. Moo, and Leon Morris, *An Introduction to the New Testament* (Grand Rapids: Zondervan, 1992), 438.

[28]. Ibid., 378.

what believers should look for in the last days and so it is no surprise that similarities appear.

Comparing 2 Timothy 3 with 2 Peter 3

Second Timothy 3		Second Peter 3	
Vs 1	Know this also… that in the last days… perilous times shall come.	Vs 3	Knowing this first… that there shall come in the last days…
Vs 2	For men shall be lovers of their own selves… boasters…		…scoffers, walking after their own lust,
Vs 7	Ever learning and never able to come to the knowledge of the truth.	Vs 5	For this they willingly are ignorant of,…

Notice that both Paul and Peter wanted the believer to know something about the last days as they assume that a discerning student of God's Word will have a sincere desire to be watching for the return of the Lord and thus looking for whatever signs of His coming the Scriptures allow. They both use the Greek word *ginosko* (to know), although in different forms. Paul wrote *touto de ginoske* or (moreover know this) and Peter wrote *ginoskontes* (know or recognize this first).[29]

Although they had wide differences in their education, Peter mostly an uneducated man, as the rulers of the Temple pointed out *"Now when they saw the boldness of Peter and John, and perceived that they were unlearned and ignorant men…"* (Acts 4:13). Paul on the other hand was a very educated man, with what would be considered a degree in Old Testament studies today. And they both had a teachers heart for the reader.

---

[29]. Albert Garner, *General Epistles*, Baptist Commentary (Lakeland, FL: Blessed Hope Foundation, 1985), 123.

Paul wanted his reader to know that the last days would be difficult and says they will be "*perilous*" days which is sometimes translated as "*grievous*". This conveys a sense of uncertainty, anxiousness, even a degree of dread. It will be a time of sin on the increase and mankind looking to God for answers on the decrease. The passage paints the picture of mankind slipping into ungodliness and thus condemnation with a boastful spirit. But instead of even the outskirts of religion providing a restraint, man will be on a degenerating path of moving away from God and soon forming an outright opposition to that which is good.

Peter wanted his reader to know that these who have gone away from God will begin questioning those who still believe in anything the Bible says. They will not only not want to be religious themselves but will become "*scoffers*" as Peter states and "despisers of those that are good" as Paul says. And Peter goes on to say that those scoffers will be "*walking after their own lusts*" (2 Peter 3:3). And that goes right along with what Paul says as he states that men "*shall be lovers of their own selves, covetous…*" (2 Timothy 3:2).

Peter says in his text in verse 5 that the scoffers are "*willingly ignorant*" which means they willingly allow the truth to escape them.[30] Compared to what Paul says, it is like the passage in 2 Timothy is giving a description of scoffers. Paul says in the last days, that the unsaved will be "*boasters*", "*proud*", "*blasphemers*", "*heady*", and "*highminded*". It is passages like this that amaze me as I see that though these two men were quite different, it was the same Holy Spirit of God that inspired them.

Where to Place These Passages in a Revelation Timeline

And so now that the similarities between these two passages have been shown, as well as how they each help in understanding each other, where would they be placed for chronologically reading through end times passages or teaching through Revelation?

---

[30]. Spence and Excell, 66.

A great place to put them is at the end of Revelation 3 but before Revelation 4 begins. Revelation chapters 2 and 3 are not only literal messages to the seven churches of John's day but also are a church history timeline, although there are many variations of the actual dates that people think they represent.[31] Notice the following chart showing not only an assigned date range that each of the seven churches of Revelation represents but that the last church, being the church of Laodicea, has no end date assigned as most pre-tribulationists believe that it goes into the Tribulation, meaning that not only was it present during the last days but was mostly not raptured, meaning that most of its congregants were not even believers. But before we place the last days between Revelation 3 and 4, let's look at the passage where the Lord is talking to the church of Laodicea in Revelation 3.

7 Stages of Church History

Church	Era	Years
Ephesus	Apostolic Era	33-64
Smyrna	Period of Persecution	64-313
Pergamum	Era of Official Patronage	313-606
Thyatira	Middle Ages	606-1520
Sardis	Protestant Reformation	1520-1750
Philadelphia	Missionary Era	1750-1900
Laodicea	Modern Period	1900-?

Seven stages of church history: This shows how Jesus is omniscient in listing the churches of John's day, knowing what they were going through and outlining church history from John's day to the last days.

---

[31]. "The Church in Prophetic Perspective," Grace to You, https://www.gty.org/library/study-guides/40-5115/the-church-in-prophetic-perspective (accessed March 10, 2016).

And some similarities may even become evident between the church of Laodicea and the rest of the world in the last days from 2 Timothy 3.

2 Timothy 3:1-9	Revelation 3:14-19
Vs 5 Having a form of godliness…	Vs 15 thou are neither cold nor hot
Vs 2 men shall be…covetous	Vs 17 thou sayest I am rich
Vs 2 men shall be…boasters, proud	Vs 17 and have need of nothing
Vs 7 never able to come to the knowledge of the truth	Vs 17 thou are blind and naked

It should come as no surprise that the world creeps into some churches and just as the Apostle Paul described the world in the last days, so did the Lord Jesus find an evidence of those same problems in the church of the last days.

Another reason for placing the Last Days passages at the end of Revelation 3 but before Revelation 4, would be an argument of absence, meaning that from Revelation 4 onward, the church is not mentioned as being present on earth until the end of the Tribulation.

There is a great argument for the last days being at the end of Revelation 3 along with the Rapture, as another chapter shall discuss. It's because of how John presents Revelation. He writes in the first chapter a sort of an outline *"Write the things which thou hast seen, and the things which are, and the things which shall be hereafter"* (Revelation 1:19). And so if the outline breaks could be determined, it would lay out the book of Revelation.

Many interpret the above passage, in referring to that outline, with "the things which are" being the present church age from Christ to the Rapture and "the things which shall be hereafter" being the events that happen after the Rapture.[32] An argument for that point would be that Revelation chapter four begins with *"After this"*, and readers should ask 'After what', and

---

[32]. Gerald B. Stanton, *Kept from the Hour* (Miami Springs, FL: Schoettle, 1991), 199.

the conclusion of most Bible believing theologians take is that the Apostle John is now recording what is happening after the rapture or after the church age is over.

For those who want to place the Rapture further into the Book of Revelation, they simply run into too many chronological problems. Using some simple logic, let's just see when the Rapture must take place. Of course, it's before the Marriage Supper of the Lamb in Revelation 19, which rules out post-millennialism. The passage in 2 Thessalonians 2:3-10 establishes that the church is raptured before the appearance of the Antichrist, which rules out post/mid-tribulationalism, as the Antichrist appears before Revelation 13. And in the comparison in a later chapter, we shall see that Revelation 6 is enlightened by Matthew 24, which means the Antichrist actually appears in Revelation 6:1, meaning the Rapture has to take place before that.[33] And that rules out the Mid-Trib or Pre-wrath view.

I agree that the view of the Lord coming to call the church home (the rapture) before the seven year Tribulation is not plainly seen by some, but when the Scriptures simply eliminate all the other possibilities, then what is simplest is likely the answer.

So when Revelation chapter four opens with crowned elders clothed in white raiment, it can be said with some certainty that those elders are the raptured church. And that is another interesting chapter to come.

---

[33]. Ibid., 264.

Chapter 7
The Gathering of Israel and the Rebuilding of the Jewish Temple

There is in Jerusalem an organization dedicated to one day rebuilding the Jewish Temple, that being the Temple Institute[34]. The Temple Institute is a private organization, operated by donations, and has been preparing for an operational Temple for years. They believe they will see the Temple built one day. They have already prepared much of the Temple furniture, have blueprints for the structure, have made some clothing for the High Priest and Levites, have a herd of red heifers at the ready and have even begun identifying which Jewish men might be qualified to serve in the Temple.

Of course, dispensationalists believe that God is not yet done with Israel and thus are very interested in these facts. And though we know that Judaism is not how one comes to God now, as it must be through Christ, we still grow excited over discussion about a restored Israel and operating Temple as we understand these things will need to take place to usher in the end times.

To initially grasp the importance of this, it is needed that we note that sometime around the beginning of the seven years of Tribulation, Israel and specifically Jerusalem come into the prophetic limelight. Every year since Herod's Temple was destroyed in 70A.D., Jews and as time went on, Christians, have looked to Israel and specifically to Jerusalem as a sign for the end times.[35] The reason is that many prophetic passages either directly or indirectly refer to the Jews gathered in Israel and the Jewish Temple standing and it seems in operation as a center of worship, just as prescribed in the Old Testament.

A look back in history, both Biblical and secular, displays the turbulent existence of the nation of Israel and its identification with the Temple on Mt. Moriah, on the north east side of Jerusalem. David, who captured Jerusalem around 1010 B.C. and made it the Jewish capital, wanted to build a permanent

---

[34]. "The Red Heifer: The Original Ashes," The Jewish Temple Institute, https://www.templeinstitute.org/red_heifer/original_ashes.htm (accessed April 23, 2016).

[35]. Randall Price, *The Coming Last Days Temple* (Eugene, OR: Harvest House, 1999), 23.

structure for worship to Jehovah, to replace the Tabernacle, which was by this time a 400 year old tent structure. And though it was his son, Solomon, who built it, David gathered materials and prepared the foundations. The Temple was completed around 962B.C. and was known as Solomon's Temple, until it was destroyed with much of the city of Jerusalem in 586B.C. by the Babylonians.[36]

The Temple had become such an important fixture, both for worship and national identity that, when some of the Jews were allowed to return to Judah and Jerusalem in 516B.C., under the care or administration of Nehemiah and Ezra, one of their main priorities was to rebuild the Temple and get it functioning again as a place of worship.[37]

And that rebuilt Temple was in existence all through the four hundred so-called 'Silent Years' or Inter-testament years, which is the time between the last book of the Old Testament and the opening of the New Testament. It's called the 'Silent Years', for though there was lots of wars and political and religious intrigue between Malachi and Matthew, there was no book of the Bible written and no prophet or preacher sent from God.

When Herod the Great came to power in 37 B.C., followed by his sons, they began remodeling the Temple which is why it became known as Herod's Temple.[38] But that Temple, which lasted through the Gospels, was destroyed in 70 A.D. by the Romans. There have been a few attempts to rebuild the Temple off and on throughout history. For instance there was interest in 130 A.D., but it seems the Romans would not support the project and another time of interest in 361 A.D but this did not work out either.[39] And so there has been no functioning Jewish Temple since 70 A.D..

With that being said, when there are prophetic passages that mention the Jewish Temple standing and mentioning worship there, it sparks the interest of those interested in prophecy. Some

---

[36]. Thomas Ice, Randall Price, and John F. Walvoord, *Ready to Rebuild: The Imminent Plan to Rebuild the Last Days Temple* (Eugene, OR: Harvest House, 1992), 51.

[37]. Randall Price, *Jerusalem in Prophecy* (Eugene, OR: Harvest House, 1998), 86.

[38]. Randall Price, *The Coming Last Days Temple*, 76.

[39]. Randall Price, *The Coming Last Days Temple*, 89.

passages portray worship to be to the Lord God Jehovah but some describe the days during the Tribulation when worship at the Jewish Temple in Jerusalem will be high-jacked by the Antichrist. It is of interest to us because if the Jewish Temple will be built and functioning during the seven years of Tribulation, then it would seem that it might be built or at least be ready to be built even before the Rapture? And so when we find the Jews in control of Jerusalem for the first time since the days of the Apostles, and a Temple Institute preparing for permission to start construction, it sure peaks our interest.

And as far as Jews being re-gathered, it is important to note that there have always been Jews living in Israel and Jerusalem, though there were many attempts to cut the connection between the Jews and their promised homeland. The Romans, Muslims, Crusaders, Ottomans, and even the British, all to one degree or another, have tried to carry them away as captives or at least limit the return of the Jews to Palestine.

On this point, there have been several dispersions or expulsions of the Jews from Israel. The first is recorded in the Biblical history of the Jews when the northern kingdom fell in 722 B.C. *"And the King of Assyria did carry away Israel unto Assyria and put them in Halah and in Habor by the river of Gozan, and in the cities of the Medes"* (2 Kings 18:11). This is the source of the 'Ten Lost Tribes' phrase, which we will deal with later. The second was the Babylonian captivity and happened during the course of several years, with several rounds of deportation, culminating in even the poor being carried away, around 587 B.C. *"Then Nebuzaradan the captain of the guard carried away captive certain of the poor of the people…"* (Jeremiah 52:15).

Later the Romans dispersed the Jews from all of Palestine because of the rebellion in 67-73A.D. and again in 136A.D., because of another rebellion. And both the Muslims and Crusaders, each wanting control of Jerusalem for religious reasons, either slew the Jews or confiscated their lands and houses, thus forcing them to relocate. And later on in modern history, to some degree the Ottomans and the British either discouraged or at least limited Jews in Jerusalem.

And so when the Jews started returning to Palestine in the 1930's and even more in the 1940's and 1950's and Israel declared itself a nation, it peaked interest in the prophetic passages that seem to only be possible if Israel was a nation. Especially with certain Biblical texts in mind like "*...from all the lands whither he had driven them; and I will bring them again into their land that I gave unto their fathers*" (Jeremiah 16:15).

The population of Jews in Israel is now over eight million but there are another ten million Jews that live outside the nation of Israel and for those who take Biblical prophecy literally, it seems obvious that when the Bible says that Israel will be re-gathered, that it is an event that still needs to take place. And the Bible speaks of this in many passages. But that doesn't mean that we can't still be interested that God is beginning to bring His chosen people home. The below chart of population growth shows that after the Roman and Muslim occupations, that hardly any Jews lived in Israel and that the population has grown to what it is now, is simply a miracle.

Table 1. Approximate Population of Jews in Israel in History

Year	Population of Jews	Year	Population of Jews
1517	5,000	1948	806,000
1882	24,000	1949	1,174,000
1918	60,000	1971	3,121,000
1931	174,000	1974	3,422,000

Source: Data from "Demographics of Israel: Jewish & Non-Jewish Population of Israel/Palestine (1517 – Present)" (November 30, 2017).

Isaiah wrote "*And it shall come to pass in that day, that the Lord shall set His hand again the second time to recover the remnant of His people, which shall be left, from Assyria, and from Egypt, and from Pathros, and from Cush, and from Elam, and from Shinar, and from Hamath, and from the islands of the sea. And He shall set up an ensign for the nations, and shall assemble the outcasts of Israel, and gather together the dispersed of Judah from the four corners of the earth*" (Isaiah 11:11-12).

Notice first, that this cannot be Moses leading the children of Israel out of Egypt into the promised land as the Lord uses the term "remnant". And it cannot be referring to the re-gathering during the times of Ezra and Nehemiah as this is stated as a "second time", the return of the captives from Assyria and Babylon would have been the first time. Also notice that the above passage conveys that this will be a global re-gathering using the phrases "*from the islands of the sea*" and "*from the four corners of the earth*". So the return of the Jews from Babylon under Zerubbabel in Nehemiah 7 and the return of another group from Shushan in Persia under Nehemiah in Nehemiah 1, could not have been this world wide gathering.

So by process of elimination, the gathering that Isaiah is talking about is an end time gathering. And the countries that are initially listed have already started to prove that. Up until the last fifty years, there were large Jewish populations in Egypt, Iraq (Assyria), Iran (Elam), and Syria (Hamath).[40] And passages on this appear all throughout the Scriptures. Notice the comparison below.

Ezekiel 37:21	Hosea 3:4	Zechariah 10:9-10
"…I will take the children of Israel from among the heathen, whither they gone and will gather them on every side and and bring them into their own land"	"For the children of Israel shall abide many days without a king…and without a sacrifice (temple) and without an image…ephod… teraphim. Afterward shall the children of Israel return…in the latter days"	"And I will sow them among the people and they shall remember me in far countries…I will bring them out of the land of Egypt and gather them out of Assyria and I will bring them into the land of Gilead…"

As of recent years, Islamic extremism has driven many Jews out of long term communities, like the one in Yemen that

---

[40]. James Rochford, "The Regathering of Israel," Evidence Unseen, http://www.evidenceunseen.com/articles/prophecy/the-regathering-of-israel/ (Accessed April 11, 2016).

has fled to Israel in 2017 or even the beginning of Jews leaving France because of increased terrorism there.

But even with these beginnings of Jews moving back to the promised land, the passages above make it clear that in the End Times, it will be worldwide. So it is clear that Israel will be brought back into the land but now the question is when? Most do not think this is a one-time event and some seem to hint that it may be a process as the earth moves towards the last days.[41] And some of the things that the prophet Hosea pointed out give a few more indications that the re-gathering will be connected to rebuilding the Jewish Temple.

Notice in the passage from Hosea 3 that they will be "without a king…or prince" meaning they will not have a political ruler. It could be argued that they currently do as in the prime minister of Israel, but that has only been since 1948, showing they did not have one for nineteen hundred years.

But in much of Israel's history it was often the religious leader, priest or prophet, that was seen to represent the people. And without a Temple, there can be no high priest. And the passage says they would be "without sacrifice" obviously stating that there would be no operational Temple. And they would not have an "ephod" pointing to them not having a priest, and for that matter no "image" meaning they would not even have a false religion.

And many are not familiar with the New Testament passage where Jesus states that not long after His death, the Jews "*…shall fall by the edge of the sword, and shall be led away captive into all nations…until the time of the Gentiles be fulfilled*" (Luke 21:24).

As to where to place the re-gathering of Israel and the rebuilding of the Jewish Temple, it seems best to agree with D.L. Pentecost as it will likely be more of a process than an event, but one could certainly try and place the process or at least the end of the last days of the church or near the beginning of the Tribulation.

One could start with the verse talking about the signing of a covenant between Israel and the Antichrist. Now, the fact that

---

[41]. Pentecost, 280.

Israel is already a nation and can sign treaties may seem old news, but it is such a wonderful fulfillment of prophecy, that it should not be ignored. The prophet Daniel made that very clear *"And he shall confirm the covenant with many for one week: and in the midst of the week he shall cause the sacrifice to cease…"* (Daniel 9:27). And in this verse, there is at least, a partial re-gathered Israel at the beginning of the seven year tribulation and clearly, a rebuilt temple in Jerusalem.

How can we conclude that? In using a little of the logic that was used to place the Rapture, let's try to at least see if we can determine when Israel will be in the land. Israel will sign the treaty with the Antichrist to start the seven years of tribulation, which means the Antichrist is known. That would mean the church has already been taken "out of the way" as Paul told the Thessalonians. But since the treaty starts the seven years of tribulation, that means the signing of the treaty is basically the start of the tribulation with the appearance of the Antichrist *"And I saw and behold a white horse and he that sat him had a bow and a crown was given to him and he went forth to conquer"* (Revelation 6:2).

So though the gathering of Israel may be currently taking place, the treaty itself will be signed somewhere between the end of Revelation 3 and the start of Revelation 6. And though the materials are being collected for the Temple, it would be likely that the building of the Temple coincided with the treaty. It is interesting that there is no mention of the Temple being in operation before the Rapture and its first mention is when the Antichrist defiles it at the three and a half year mark.

In conclusion, it seems that there are several pieces of the puzzle that need to fall into place before Israel can fulfill its Tribulation prophecies. God is not an author of confusion and it is my opinion that the church must be gone before Israel comes on the stage of God's plan again. Again, time will tell!

Chapter 8
The Rapture of the Saints

      One of the most comforting topics to the New Testament Christian is called the Rapture. While the word "rapture" is not in English translations, it is the Latin verb "rapere", which means 'to seize', 'to transport', or 'to call away' and is Latin for the phrase "shall be caught up" in 1 Thessalonians 4:17. So when someone might say that the word Rapture is not in modern Bibles, someone could politely disagree and say that it is in the Latin Bible but it has been conveniently translated into English for them.

      The word Rapture is commonly used to describe the Bible doctrine of the gathering of the saints to Christ at His Second Advent. This takes place at the end of the church age and in the Pre-Tribulation Rapture view before the Tribulation, as the Lord promises to keep the church "*from the hour of temptation*" (Revelation 3:10).

      After the Lord appears in the clouds to call up the Christians, they are then taken to heaven. There are several groups of believers in the Scriptures, not that they were saved necessarily in a different way, but in different dispensations and the Rapture is referring to those saved during the church age.[42]

      As already mentioned, the most famous passage on the subject of the Rapture is in 1 Thessalonians 4:13-18, where the Apostle Paul seems to be answering questions that were of great concern to the early church. The questions seem to center around if a believer died, did that mean they would miss the Rapture and thus miss being able to go to heaven or at the least, there was a concern that those saints that died would have a disadvantage in going to heaven at the return of Christ, likely the beginnings of the heresy of soul sleep. Paul lays these concerns to rest by stating "*the dead in Christ shall rise first*" (1 Thessalonians 4:16).

      And only after the saints which had died in Christ have risen, then those saints which remain shall rise "*Then we which are alive and remain shall be caught up together with them in the*

---

[42]. Pentecost, 199.

clouds, to meet the Lord in the air and so shall we ever be with the Lord" (1 Thessalonians 4:17). But 1 Thessalonians is not the only passage that covers the topic of the Rapture. 1 Corinthians 15 does also but is more than just an answer to some questions for it seems that the 1 Corinthians passage is part of a larger topic, intending to teach the believer several things concerning the resurrection of the New Testament believer. So let's consider some similarities and some lessons drawn from both of these passages.

1 Corinthians 15		1 Thessalonians 4	
vs 51	Behold I show you a mystery…	vs 13	But I would not have you to be ignorant…
vs 52	At the last trump, for the trumpet shall sound…the dead shall be raised…	vs 16	…with the trump of God …the dead in Christ shall rise...
vs 58	…be ye stedfast, unmoveable… as ye know that your labor is not in vain in the Lord.	vs 18	Wherefore comfort one another with these words.

    In the Corinthians passage, Paul speaks of the church as a mystery, known only by Divine revelation. It is important to note that it is not the resurrection that is the mystery but the church. And in Thessalonians, he refers to those who do not know about the rapture as "*ignorant*" or uninformed. This seems to point to the simple fact that the 'Church' was just not seen in prophecy by the Old Testament saints. But we must remember that they were mostly Jews and the prophetic promises made to them were about the nation of Israel, not the church age, where God would call and save Gentiles to His name.

    Also notice that both passages teach that the church, or those who will be taken in the Rapture are "*in Christ*". Notice the following similarities in how Paul refers to the saved as those "*in Christ*" or "*in Jesus*".

1 Corinthians 15		1 Thessalonians 4	
vs 2	Ye which are saved…	vs 13	Brethren…
vs 18	Then they also which are fallen asleep in Christ…	vs 14	…even so them also which sleep in Jesus

When a believer is "*in Christ*" or "*in Jesus*", he or she is counted righteous by Christ's righteousness and thus saved. And Paul makes it very clear in both passages, that those who are truly saved will be taken in the Rapture and changed at the resurrection.[43] There is also a difference between those who profess to be saved and those who are actually "born again" (John 3:3) for only those truly "in Christ" or truly saved and part of the true church will be raptured.[44] To know of Christ, to know about Christ, to even follow Christ is not the requirement as Paul says we must be in Christ's redemption.

The Rapture is a resurrection of the New Testament saints but it is not what some call the general resurrection but specifically for New Testament Christians. This seems clear from 1 Corinthians 15:23 which informs readers that those "who are Christ's" will be raised. Old Testament saints will be resurrected at the end of the Tribulation when the Lord physically comes to earth to set up His kingdom and fulfill all the promises made to the Old Testament saints. And there is somewhat of a resurrection at the end of the Millennium when all the unsaved dead will be brought before the Great White Throne as described in Revelation 19. But the Rapture is exclusive to those who have died or are living at the time of the Lord's call having trusted in Christ for their salvation from the cross until the Rapture.

Another wonderful truth about the one day Rapture of the saints is that when Christ returns from heaven to call the Christians home, is that believers will be changed, both

---

[43]. John Piper, *Counted Righteous in Christ? Should We Abandon the Imputation of Christ's Righteousness?* (Wheaton: Crossway Books, 2002) 54-55.

[44]. Pentecost, 199.

physically, emotionally, mentally and spiritually. Literally anything and everything that is flawed from the fall of mankind into sin in the Garden of Eden is reversed and made perfect.

And both the 1 Corinthians 15 passage and Philippians 3 speak of that.

1 Corinthians 15	Philippians 3
vs 51 ...we shall not all sleep but we shall all be changed	vs 21 Who shall change our vile body ...that it may be fashioned like unto His glorious body...
vs 52 ...and we shall be changed	
vs 42 ...it is raised in incorruption	
vs 43 ...it is raised in glory	
vs 44 ...it is raised a spiritual body	

As for the details of the Rapture, there are several things that are known. In 1 Thessalonians 4:15 Paul states it is at *"the coming (parousia) of the Lord"*. This is when *"the Lord Himself will descend from heaven with a shout (cry of command), with the voice of the archangel, and with the trumpet of God"* (v. 16). And this trumpet is called the last trumpet according to 1 Corinthians 15:52, meaning the start of the last days trumpets or perhaps the last trumpet for the church. On this occasion the saints are caught up in the clouds *"to meet the Lord in the air, and thus we shall ever be with the Lord"* (1 Thess. 4:17).

Below shows where the Rapture would occur in relation to other end time events. It is at the end of the last days of the church but before the appearance of the Anti-christ and seven year Tribulation.

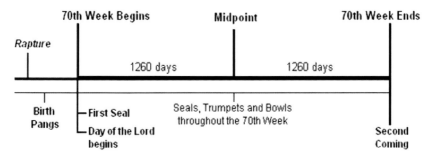

Pre-Tribulation rapture timeline.

As to whether New Testament Christians will know the timing of the Rapture is the topic of a lot of discussion. Christians are told very clearly by the Lord Jesus that "*of that day and hour knoweth no man, no, not the angels of heaven, but my Father only*" (Matthew 24:36) and many have foolishly tried to predict when the Lord would return.

But does that mean that the discerning Christian who is alive in the end times will not see signs of the Lord's impending return, even if he cannot pin down a date? As mentioned before, the Apostle Paul seems to say that the discerning Christian will be able to see the signs of the Lord's soon return. He writes "*But of the times and the seasons, brethren, ye have no need that I write unto you. For yourselves know perfectly that the day of the Lord cometh as a thief in the night*" (1 Thessalonians 5:1-2). And Paul goes on to say "*But ye brethren, are not in darkness, that that day should overtake you as a thief*" (1 Thessalonians 5:4). And so even referring to what the Lord said, why watch if there is nothing to see!

But while it is clear that the discerning believer in the last days might be able to look for signs of the Lord's return, there is also a sense of surprise and immanency. Paul told those same believers at Thessalonica "*the day of the Lord so cometh as a thief in the night*" (1 Thessalonians 5:2) and the Lord Jesus said the same thing to His disciples "*Watch therefore: for ye know not what hour your Lord doth come*" (Matthew 24:42). So because of these and other Scriptures, there is the doctrine of the imminent return of Christ, which in plain language means that He may appear at any moment.[45]

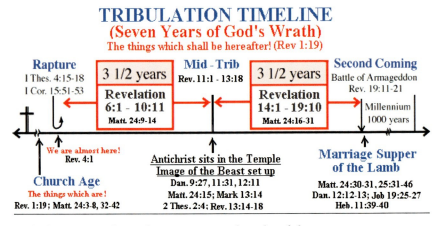

Tribulation timeline showing some details of those seven years.

The word *imminent* can be rendered *impending*, and some have used the word *overhanging* which gives a certain feel of something that may come very fast. Applying this meaning to the Rapture, Gerald Stanton said in his book that it means three things.

First, it would clearly mean the certainty of the Lord's return. If something is imminent, it is too close to not happen. Secondly, there is a certain uncertainty about the timing of the event. So even though it may seem close, there is an unknown aspect, like it is around the corner and may or may not be here any moment. And Stanton also says imminent, on the topic of the Rapture, means that there is nothing that stands in the way of the event happening, by that meaning there are no known prophetic events that believers are waiting on, no unfilled Scripture that has yet to be fulfilled.[46]

As to where in the chronological timeline one would place teaching on the Rapture, it would come after the last days but before the Tribulation. Another comparison of Scripture that

---

[45]. Stanton, 109.

[46]. Stanton, 108.

is helpful in the timing of the Rapture is to look at the two last churches of Revelation 2-3.

The sixth church, the church of Philadelphia seems to be a Bible believing church that is trying to win people to Christ while the church of Laodicea in Revelation seems to be a church in name only and is often seen as the unsaved church that is not taken in the Rapture and goes into the Tribulation. Is that is true, then we should see a stark contrast between the two. And if there is, the Rapture could be placed at the end of Revelation 3.

The Church of Philadelphia Revelation 3		The Church of Laodicea Revelation 3	
vs 8	…behold I have set before thee an open door…	vs 20	Behold I stand at the door and knock…
	…thou has a little strength	vs 17	…thou are wretched and miserable and poor…
	…thou has kept my word and has not denied my name	vs 18	I counsel thee to buy of me gold tried in the fire…
vs 9	…I have loved thee	vs 16	I will spue thee out of my mouth
vs 10	Because thou hast kept my word	vs 15	…thou art neither cold nor hot
	…I also will keep thee from the hour of temptation…	vs 19	…I rebuke and chasten…
vs 11	Behold I come quickly…	vs 19	…therefore repent

So the contrast is very clear. The church of Philadelphia has an open door or access to the Lord's work and ways and rewards, while the church of Laodicea's door is closed and the Lord is having to knock to gain admission.

Philadelphia has some strength because it was faithful while Laodicea is called wretched and miserable and poor. The Lord tells the church at Philadelphia they have been persecuted for not denying His name while the church at Laodicea needs to still go through persecution in the fire.

The Lord tells Philadelphia that He loves them and tells Laodicea that He will spue them out of His mouth. Philadelphia is told that they have been very faithful in keeping the Lord's word while Laodicea is fickle and neither hot or cold.

The believers at Philadelphia are told they will be kept from the hour, which must be referring to the Rapture while the people in the church at Laodicea will be rebuked and chastened. And the Lord tells the church of Philadelphia that He will come quickly while the church of Laodicea is not ready for Him at all and needs to repent. The contrast is clear!

Another reason that the Rapture should be placed near the end of Revelation three is that by chapter four, the true church is in heaven, represented by the elders "And round about the throne were four and twenty seats and upon the seats I saw four and twenty elders sitting…" (Revelation 4:4).[47]

The reasons to view these "elders" as the church are many. The word "seats" in the King James can be translated as "thrones" and while the New Testament believer is promised to rule and reign with Christ *"we shall also reign with Him"* (2 Timothy 2:12). Also worth noting is that these elders are clothed in white raiment, again something promised to the New Testament believer *"which have not defiled their garments and they shall walk with me in white"* (Revelation 3:4).

These elders also have crowns. Now the Old Testament saint, though just as righteous by their belief looking forward to the Messiah, was never promised a crown, and in fact, were supposed to be loyal to the king wearing the crown. To them, to wear a crown would almost seem disloyal to the line of David. But in contrast, the New Testament believer is promised several crowns as a reward for different areas of faithfulness or service to Christ.[48] There are around five crowns mentioned in the New Testament as rewards. One is for staying pure, which could be for both Old and New Testament believer but it is mentioned in 1

---

[47]. Pentecost, 207.

[48]. LaHaye and Ice, *Charting the End Times*, 55.

Corinthians. One crown is for an elder and again could be both Old and New Testament but it is mentioned in 1 Peter.

But the other three are exclusively New Testament recipients. One is called the Soul Winner's Crown "*For what is our hope or joy or crown of rejoicing…*" (1 Thessalonians 2:19). Another is for those who look forward to the Lord's coming, obviously exclusively for the New Testament saint "*There is laid up for me a crown of righteousness…unto all them also that love His appearing*" (2 Timothy 4:8). And the other is the martyrs crown, which could only be for those who give their life for Christ "*…be faithful unto death and I will give thee a crown of life*" (Revelation 2:10).

Chapter 9
The Judgment Seat of Christ

The Judgment Seat of Christ, also known as the Bema Seat, the Greek word being *Bema*, happens after the New Testament saints are taken to heaven in the Rapture. It is an event described in Scripture where all those saved from the cross to the Rapture are judged or evaluated by Christ regarding their life on earth. It seems that there will be rewards for a variety of actions and characteristics, from acts of loyalty to acts of kindness. Some equate the rewards to crowns and list a set number based on specific verses that mention five crowns that shall be given to believers.[49]

1 Cor. 9:25	Rev. 2:10	1 Peter 5:2-4	2 Timothy 4:8	1 Thess. 2:19
"Every man that striveth for the mastery is temperate in all things. Now they do it to obtain a corruptible *crown* but we an incorruptible"	"Fear none of those things which thou shall suffer…and ye shall have tribulation ten days; be thou faithful unto death and I will give thee a *crown* of life"	"Feed the flock of God which is among you, taking the over-sight thereof… And when the chief Shepherd shall appear, ye shall receive a *crown* of glory that fadeth not"	"There is laid up for me a *crown* of right-eousness which the Lord, the righteous judge shall give me at that day and not to me only but unto all them also that love his appearing"	"For what is our hope or joy or *crown* of rejoicing? Are not even ye in the presence of our Lord Jesus Christ at His coming?"

---

[49]. LaHaye and Ice, *Charting the End Times*, 54.

The above passages mention:

1) **The Victor's Crown**, which is usually described as the reward given to those who live for the Lord, or have some victory over sin or a selfish life. They put the temptations of the world aside in order to be profitable for the cause of Christ and will one day receive an incorruptible crown, given the name to be in contrast to the corruptible things of the world that they gave up.

2) **The Crown of Life** is often called the "martyr's crown" and Tim LaHaye refers to it as the "the sufferers crown" as it seems to directly intend on compensating for the injustices in life.[50] And LaHaye also says that it is to purposely reward those who the Lord addresses when He says *"Fear none of those things which thou shalt suffer: behold the devil shall cast some of you into prison, that ye may be tried; and ye shall have tribulation ten days: be thou faithful unto death and I will give thee a crown of life"* (Revelation 2:10).

3) **The Crown of glory** is usually called the Elders crown or the Shepherds crown or the Pastor's crown and is for those who have faithfully taught God's Word to God's people.

4) **The Crown of Righteousness** is for those believers who have lived a righteous and holy life because they were looking and yearning for the Lord's return. It is a reward for those who sincerely love the Lord Jesus and cannot wait to see Him and be with Him. And because they eagerly await Jesus' return, while they live in this world, they are unattached to it and long to be in the next life with Christ.

5) **The Crown of Rejoicing** is the 'Soul winners' crown and is for those who share the Gospel with the purpose of planting seeds of salvation and for those who then cultivate those seeds and for those who bring them to life and lead people to a saving knowledge of Christ. And whether it be the lonely missionary or the unseen Sunday school teacher, one day all those who have

---

[50]. LaHaye and Ice, *Charting the End Times*, 54.

been part of seeing souls saved from the clutches of satan shall be rewarded.

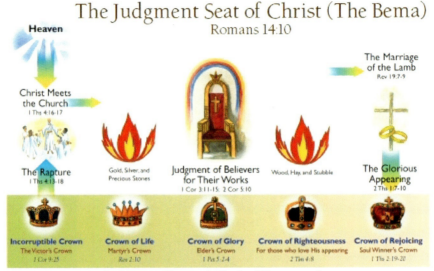

Judgment Seat of Christ Illustrated

While it seems very certain that awarding the crowns is certainly part of this time when we stand before Christ, others look at the Judgment Seat of Christ with a wider view. And I think rightly so, as there may be all sorts of rewards given for all sorts of things done in Christ's name. But not first without an in-depth examination before the Son of God.[51]

For though one aspect of the judgment seat is definitely sort of a rewards ceremony, there is certainly an aspect that some will have to give an account for their lack of effort for the Lord or see that some things were done with the wrong motive, and not count as works done for Christ.

It does seem clear that our sins will not be what is brought up but perhaps missed opportunities. The judgment time will not be about sins of commission but about sins of omission.

There are three passages that are clearly connected to concerning the Judgment Seat of Christ. And they each add

---

[51]. Pentecost, 219.

something that helps us with understanding it. So let's compare Scripture again to see what it teaches believers.

Romans 14:12	1 Corinthians 3:13	2 Corinthians 5:10
"So then every one of us shall give account of himself to God"	"Every man's work shall be made manifest: for the day shall declare it, because it shall be revealed by fire; and the fire shall try every man's work of what sort it is"	"For we must all appear before the judgment seat of Christ; that every one may receive the things done in his body, according to that he hath done, whether it be good or bad"

First, notice the clear fact that every Christian will one day give an account. The book of Romans reads *"every one of us"*, 1 Corinthians says *"every man's work"*, and 2 Corinthians uses the phrase *"we must **all** appear"*. In his book *Kept From The Hour*, Stanton uses this as one of his proofs for a pre-tribulational rapture, as the judgment is for all believers.[52] The point would be that if all New Testament Christians are going to be judged at the Bema Seat, and since it would need to be before the Marriage supper of the Lamb, that it must be either before the Tribulation or at least early in those seven years.

Second, notice that this will be a time of detailed inspection. Romans uses the word *"account"*, 1 Corinthians says that each one's "work shall be made manifest" and 2 Corinthians makes it clear that rewards will be based "according to that he hath done". Dwight Pentecost states that this is not a judgment to determine whether people are believers or not, but it is believers' works that are brought into judgment or review.[53] He also argues that this judgment will not deal with sin as *"their sins and iniquities will I remember no more"* (Hebrews 10:17) but an

---

[52]. Stanton, 72.

[53]. Pentecost, 222.

inspection of deeds and under what motive and attitude they were done or why some act of obedience was not done.

Third, it is clear that the judge will be the Lord Jesus Himself. Though Romans uses the word "God", notice that it is not 'God the Father', but "God", referring to the Divine One, which can be Jesus, as He is part of the Trinity. And 2 Corinthians uses the phrase "*judgment seat of Christ*", making it clear that it belongs to and is ran by Christ. And even the Lord Jesus Himself spoke of this "*For the Father judgeth no man, but hath committed all judgment unto the Son*" (John 5:22).

Fourthly, not all things done in the name of Christ or in Christian service are going to be rewarded. The book of Romans states that believers "shall give an account himself" and what besides good efforts and good deeds would need an explanation? There would be no arguments over sinful actions or wrong deeds but there will be discrepancy over the things a believer may think will be rewarded and those things which will not.

It is well known that men enjoy passing judgment upon one another but in this case all are accountable to God.[54] The 1 Corinthians passage says that "every man's work shall be made manifest" or clear. And that could only be if from this side of the eternity, it is not always known what goes on behind the scenes. And the 1 Corinthians passage says it will be "revealed by fire". This really comes to light from the preceding verse "*Now if any man build upon this foundation gold, silver, precious stones, wood, hay, stubble*" (1 Corinthians 3:12), the foundation being Christ, but notice that not everything built or done for Christ will survive fire.

This can remind the reader of where the Lord Jesus told the church at Laodicea to "*buy of me gold tried in the fire*" (Revelation 3:18). And then the 2 Corinthians passage uses the phrase "*whether it be good or bad*". So if this cannot be to answer for outright sin, since all sin was paid for at the cross, then it must be to answer for motive and purpose and perhaps even effectiveness in doing good deeds and use of resources that the Lord entrusted to believers. Wouldn't that even be taught by the Lord's parable of the Talents, where His servants were

---

[54]. Spence and Exell, 414.

rewarded or chastised based on what they had accomplished for Him.

And fifth, notice the time or tense of this event. Romans says "shall", in future tense and since it also said "every one of us", meaning all Christians, the "shall" must be referring to a future event beyond the age of the church. 1 Corinthians also uses the word "shall" but goes to say "for that day shall", which to those who study prophetic passages, immediately makes them think of the "day of the Lord" which uses the word "day" many times over to talk about the end times, like when Paul wrote to the Thessalonians "*For yourselves know perfectly that the day of the Lord so cometh as a thief in the night*" (1 Thessalonians 5:2).

And 2 Corinthians says that "we must all appear before the judgment seat of Christ", which makes clear again that the judgment cannot happen until all the Christians are in heaven. And Paul said "*judge nothing before the time*" (1 Corinthians 4:5), referring to being careful about coming to conclusions before the end of the age has been fulfilled.

As to what will be rewarded besides the specific items that warrant a crown, there is likely a long list as the Lord knows all things, but one can glean from Scripture some passages that focus on some specific areas that though may not promise a crown but that do promise a reward.

1) Praying will be rewarded as Jesus said "*But thou, when thou prayest, enter into thy closest and when thou hast shut thy door, pray to thy Father which is in secret; and thy Father which seeth in secret shall reward thee openly*" (Matthew 6:6).

2) The Lord promises to reward, if done right, fasting and says "*But thou, when thou fastest, anoint thine head, and wash thy face: that thou appear not unto men to fast, but unto thy Father which is in secret: and thy Father which seeth in secret, shall reward thee openly*" (Matthew 6:17-18).

3) Believers are promised that when they have compassion for the vulnerable, specifically their brothers and sisters in the Lord, the Lord will reward them as the Bible says "*Then shall the righteous answer him saying, Lord, when saw we thee an*

hungered and fed thee or thirsty and gave thee drink? When saw we thee a stranger and took thee in or naked and clothed thee? Or when saw we thee sick or in prison and came unto thee? And the King shall answer and say unto them, Verily I say unto you, Inasmuch as ye have done it unto one of the least of these my brethren, ye have done it unto me" (Matthew 25:37-40).

4) Believers are promised great reward when they bear insults or exclusion as a result of their identifying with Christ. The Lord said *"Blessed are you when men shall hate you, and when they shall separate you from their company, and shall reproach you and cast out your name as evil, for the Son of man's sake. Rejoice ye in that day, and leap for joy: for behold your reward is great in heaven…"* (Luke 6:22-23). It seems odd to "rejoice" and "leap for joy" when persecuted but Jesus said to do that exact thing, for if that happens, the person evidently has just accumulated some rewards in heaven.

5) Jesus also promises a great reward when believers love their enemies as He said *"But love your enemies and do good, and lend, hoping for nothing again; and your reward shall be great, and ye shall be the children of the Highest: for he is kind unto the unthankful and to the evil"* (Luke 6:35). This is not just for being persecuted but for responding in kindness to those who insult or try to hurt others. Though it may not often be thought of, when believers love their enemies, they are acting like Christ, for even on the cross, Jesus said *"Father, forgive them for they know not what they do"* (Luke 23:24.

6) There is reward for those who give generously. Jesus promises that when He said *"Give and it shall be given unto you; good measure, pressed down, and shaken together, and running over, shall men give into your bosom. For with the same measure that ye mete withal it shall be measured to you again"* (Luke 6:38). God promises to reward, and it could almost be said, reward in kind, to those who are generous with their offerings and possessions.

7) The seventh area that the Bible promises a reward for is when someone provides hospitality to someone who cannot repay them and thus, the action is pure kindness with no expectations for a return of favor. Jesus spoke of this when He said *"When thou makest a dinner or a supper, call not thy friends, nor thy brethren, neither thy kinsmen, nor thy rich neighbors; lest they also bid thee again, and a recompence be made thee. But when thou makest a feast, call the poor, the maimed, the lame, the blind: And thou shalt be blessed for they cannot recompense thee…"* (Luke 14:12-14). Every time believers go out of their way to be kind and hospitable to those who are less fortunate in some way, Jesus notices and promises to bless them.

8) There is also a promise of eternal reward for those who endure pressures in ministry. Paul wrote *"For our light affliction, which is but for a moment, worketh for us a far more exceeding and eternal weight of glory; while we look not at the things which are seen, but at the things which are not seen: for the things which are seen are temporal; but the things which are not seen are eternal"* (2 Corinthians 4:17-18). Whether the pastor who holds his tongue when unfairly criticized, the church volunteer who feels overworked in their ministry, or the Christian who endures stress because they are trying to be a faithful leader at church, God promises that there are eternal rewards in glory that are worth far more than the grief they endured here on earth.

9) Paul, in writing to the Christians in Asia Minor, encouraged them to be good employees and promised that the Lord would notice. He said *"And whatsoever you do, do it heartily, as to the Lord and not unto men; knowing that of the Lord ye shall receive the reward of the inheritance: for ye serve the Lord Christ"* (Colossians 3:23-24). How encouraging to know that even outside of church and in the secular world, the Lord notices when believers try to be good employees. This of course, like many of the other types of areas of life that Jesus promises to reward, is intended to give believers motivation to live rightly and represent Him well.

10) And lastly, at least for this list, Christians are promised a reward if they stay faithful to the truth of the Scriptures. Near the end of the apostolic era, error and wrong beliefs had already begun to creep in and so John wrote *"For many deceivers are entered into the world, who confess not that Jesus Christ is come in the flesh. This is a deceiver and an antichrist. Look to yourselves, that we lose not those things which we have wrought, but that we receive a full reward"* (2 John 1:7-8). And in today's culture, it sure is easy to see why the Lord made sure to tell believers that there is a reward for those who do not give up or give in on what the Lord has said.

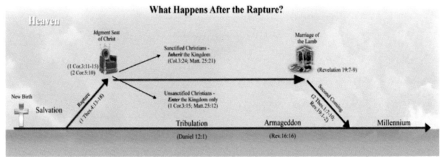

What happens after the Rapture.

As to where the Judgment Seat of Christ falls in the prophecy timeline, it can with certainty be put after the Rapture and taking place in heaven during the early start of the Tribulation on earth. The reasons are simple. The Judgment Seat of Christ is for believers and thus the Rapture has to have already taken place. And it is before the Marriage Supper of the Lamb which will last for most of the seven year Tribulation period, putting the Judgment Seat at the very beginning of the Tribulation period.

Chapter 10
The Marriage Supper of the Lamb in Heaven

The marriage supper for Christians in heaven is one of the least preached on or written about topics of prophecy, and yet it will one of the most wonderful events that ever takes place in the future life of the believer. It is a definite event, that includes all Christians, and will last for years. In this case, the beliefs held about it are not erroneous teachings or beliefs but mostly a lack of knowledge as there is hardly any teaching about it at all.

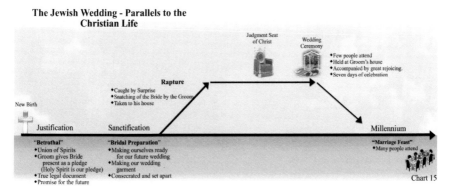

What happens at a Jewish wedding

The event is after the Rapture and following the judgment seat of Christ.[55] It is then that Christ will claim the church as His bride and then all will celebrate with a heavenly feast! And in spite of the lack of teaching by mankind, this supper seems to be one of the Lord's favorite themes in His teaching. There is the parable of the ten virgins, who were preparing for the coming of the wedding groom in Matthew 25, which we will look at later. And there is the Matthew 22 passage, where Jesus told another parable about the King sending out servants to invite them to the celebration of the marriage of His Son.

Most think that its mention by John is the first time it shows up in Scripture. John writes *"And he saith unto me, Write, Blessed are they which are called unto the marriage supper of*

---

[55]. Pentecost, 226.

the Lamb…" (Revelation 19:9). But as has briefly been shown, there are many passages that give a deeper understanding of this glorious event.

The initial passage in Revelation shows that there are actually two stages, the first being the "marriage of the Lamb" (Revelation 19:7) where the Lord takes the church as His bride, and then the "marriage supper of the Lamb" as shown above in verse 9, where there will be a great celebration. But before studying some passages in Revelation, let's compare some other verses in the Bible.

John 3:29	Ephesians 5:27	2 Corinthians 11:2
"He that hath the bridegroom but the friend of the bridegroom, which standeth and heareth him, rejoiceth greatly because of the bridegroom's voice…"	"That he might present it to Himself a glorious church, not having spot or wrinkle or any such thing…that it should be holy and without blemish"	"For I am jealous over you with godly jealousy: for I have espoused you to one husband, that I may present you as a chaste virgin to Christ"

In the three passages above it can be noted that early on in the New Testament, the concept of the Lord being viewed as the Bridegroom, the church as the Bride, and that the relationship is seen as a marriage is there. In the Gospel of John, Jesus used language to illustrate about the bride and the bridegroom and also used the subject of a wedding ceremony. In the above verse from John 3, John the Baptist was asked to identify himself and he referred to Christ as the Bridegroom and himself as just a friend who waits and listens for the Bridegrooms voice.

In Ephesians 5:27 the Apostle Paul, in speaking to husbands and wives, compares the husband to none other than Christ and the wife to the Church. And in case there was any confusion, he sums the passage up by saying in vs 32 *"This is a great mystery: but I speak concerning Christ and the church"*. So when someone gives their life to Christ, He not only saves them but they also become part of the church, which He loves as a Bridegroom loves His bride.

And as shown the Pauline Epistles are filled with more references about the church being the Bride of Christ. In fact, that happens to be a main reason, according to most theologians for the Lord needing to Rapture the church before the Tribulation[56] as what Groom would allow His bride to suffer unnecessarily.

As to where this marriage will take place, in Revelation 19:14 the Lord Jesus is coming to earth to set up His kingdom and evidently, the marriage supper or celebration has already taken place "And the armies which were in heaven followed him upon white horses, clothed in fine linen, white and clean". So in this verse, the church, already judged, accepted, rewarded and belonging to Christ, returns with Christ as He comes to set up His kingdom.[57] And since the Lord and the Bride are coming from heaven, the Marriage Supper of the Lamb can only have taken place there.

And so since the Judgment Seat of Christ takes place at the beginning of the Tribulation after the Bema Seat and since the Church comes with Christ at the end of the Tribulation, the Marriage Supper of the Lamb has to have taken place during the Tribulation in heaven. But the following will compare a few passages just to make sure.

Matthew 22:9	Revelation 19:7	Revelation 22:17
"Go ye therefore into the highways, and as many as ye shall find, bid to the marriage"	"Let us be glad and rejoice, and give honor to Him: for the marriage of the Lamb is come, and His wife hath made herself ready"	"And the Spirit and the bride say, Come, And let him that is athirst come. And whosoever will, let him take the water of life freely"

---

[56]. Stanton, 174.

[57]. Pentecost, 226.

In Matthew, Jesus is telling the parable of the wedding feast and the invitation is still being given. In Revelation 19:7, the Bridegroom and the Bride are being united and in Revelation 22:17, the Spirit of God and the Bride are speaking now together.

If one looks at Revelation 1-3 as the days of the Church Age and Revelation 4-18 as the Tribulation and then at Revelation 19 as the end of the Tribulation and the coming of Christ, and at Revelation 20-22 as the Millennium and Eternity, then the Marriage Supper of the Lamb has taken place between Revelation 4 and 18. So while the earth is enduring the wrath of God, the church will be safely in heaven with its Lord!

Chapter 11
The Four Horsemen

The Four Horsemen of the Apocalypse are described by John the Apostle when he was on the isle of Patmos in the book of Revelation. They are thought to be the first four seals that are opened on the scroll that unleashes God's judgment on the earth. There are four different colors of horses: white, red, black and pale. And each rider carries something which helps distinguish what each horsemen brings to the earth, which seems to somewhat coincide with the color of the horse. Here is a brief look at these four horsemen.

The four horsemen of the Apocalypse

Horse Color	What the Rider Had	What Happened
White	Bow and Crown	He went forth to conquer
Red	Power to take peace	Men killed one another
Black	Pair of Balances	Famine
Pale	Power to kill	War, hunger, beasts, death

Though there is not much disagreement as to the last three horsemen, there is concerning the first horseman, and that is whether the rider on the white horse is Christ or the Antichrist. It seems clear, as we shall see, that it is not Christ but the Antichrist, but some would disagree. One of the early church fathers, Irenaeus of the 2nd century first interpreted this white horse rider as Christ Himself, with His white horse representing the successful ministry of bringing the Gospel to earth. The color white could of course represent righteousness, and that comparison is found throughout the Scriptures "*Purge me with hyssop, and I shall be clean: wash me, and I shall be whiter than snow*" (Psalm 51:7).

Some have argued that the placement of the Messiah riding on the first horse with all the tribulation troubles still coming on the next three horses as inconsistent with the victorious return of Christ. But this could be explained and fairly so, by the fact that the Gospel is said to survive through difficult days and even persecutions. In fact, some would say the Lord taught that very thing "*...I will build my church and the gates of hell shall not prevail against it*" (Matthew 16:18).

However, when other prophetic passages influence the interpretation of Revelation 6, it will be clear that the white horseman can be none other than the Antichrist. To start with, a look at Revelation 5 will show that it is Jesus Himself that is opening the seals, from which the riders come, and so it would be unlikely that He is opening the seals and at the same time, was one of the seals Himself.

Revelation 5 starts off in verse 1 with the scroll in God's hand "*And I saw in the right hand of him that sat on the throne a book written within and on the backside, sealed with seven seals*". And at first, there was no one qualified to open the scroll as verse 3 states "*And no man in heaven, nor in earth, neither under the earth, was able to open the book...*". But then one of the elders, who seems to be an elder of the church, said in verse 5 "*And one of the elders saith unto me, Weep not: behold the Lion of the Tribe of Judah, the Root of David, hath prevailed to open the book and to loose the seals thereof*". Then the Lamb, who is Christ, comes and takes the scroll in verse 7 "*And He came and took the book out of the right hand of Him that sat upon the throne*". And in verse 9, Christ begins to open the scroll "...*Thou art worthy to take the book and to open the seals thereof...*".

But that is not the only argument that Christ cannot be the rider on the white horse and so the rider must be someone else, likely the Antichrist.[58] So other passages should be looked at. First, one should look at the four curses found in Leviticus 26 that God says will come upon Israel if they will not follow the Lord.

Leviticus 26	Revelation 6
vs 22 "I will also send wild beast…"	vs 2 "…and a crown was given to him and he went forth conquering and to conquer."
vs 25 "And I will bring a sword…"	vs 4 "…and there was given unto him a great sword"
vs 26 "And when I have broken the staff of your bread…	vs 5 "…A measure of wheat for a penny and three measures of barley for a penny…"
vs 25 "…I will send the pestilence…"	vs 8 "…to kill with sword and with hunger and with death and with the beasts of the earth."

So all the way back in Leviticus, God was warning Israel of tough times. And though these punishments certainly happened to them during the Old Testament times, it is very interesting just how close they match up to the outline of the four horsemen. And though in the Christian era, we don't look to Old Testament punishment passages as concerning us, during the Tribulation, the Christians are gone and God's attention has turned back to Israel.

---

[58]. Pink, 72.

The Four Sore Judgments of Eze 14:21	The Sorrows of Matthew 24	Four Curses in Leviticus 26	The First Four Seals of Revelation 6
Beasts	False Christs & Prophets	Wild Beasts	First Seal - Conquerer on a White Horse
Sword	Wars	Sword	Second Seal - Warring Rider with Sword on a Red Horse
Famine	Famine	Broken Staff of Bread	Third Seal - Rider who brings Famine on a Black Horse
Pestilence	Pestilence	Pestilence	Fourth Seal - Death and Hell on a Pale Horse

Comparison of judgments.

Another interesting comparison is found by comparing Ezekiel 14 to Revelation 6. Here the prophet Ezekiel warns Israel with almost identical language as those found in John's prophecy. It is at this point that the concept of near and far prophecy should be explained again.[59]

As earlier explained, God will sometimes lay out a prophecy where there will be partial fulfillment to some degree in the current lives of the writer or listener, and then many years later, the prophecy is totally fulfilled to such a degree and with such detail, that it is clear that God was involved as the fulfillment is simply miraculous and that there was no way that it could have happened without a Divine hand.

So comparing the Revelation 6 judgments to those mentioned in the Old Testament, one should observe that it is perhaps God laying out the punishment for Israel that will happen in the near term if them stray from Him, but then in the End Times as well. These very warnings show up in such a way that the entire world will notice, including every Jew around the world.

A reader of the New Testament and history of those times will have to recognize that God did allow the Jews to be scattered after the rejection of Christ and the punishment of Jerusalem but that God promised to bring them back again. And for this to

---

[59]. Charles Ryrie, *Ryrie Study Bible* (Chicago: Moody Press, 1994), 296.

happen, these judgments would not just be able to happen in Israel as it exist today but would need to be world-wide to get the attention of every person on earth.

So as Ezekiel wrote to the Hebrew reader, many of whom were living in forced exile in Babylon and the surrounding lands of Persia, this warning was not just for the near future but would in effect, hover over Israel for all of time. And at the last, be completely fulfilled as the Tribulation begins. So the next section will look at this comparison of prophecies…

Ezekiel 14	Revelation 6
vs 15 "If I cause <u>noisome beasts</u> to pass through the land and they spoil it, so that it be desolate…"	vs 2 "…ac a crown was given to him and he went forth conquering and to conquer."
vs 17 "Or if I bring a <u>great sword</u> upon that land…"	vs 4 "…and there was given unto him a great sword"
vs 13 "and will break the staff of bread …and will send a <u>famine</u> upon it…"	vs 5 "…A measure of wheat for a penny and three measures of barley for a penny…"
vs 19 "Or if I send <u>a pestilence</u> into land and pour out my fury…"	vs 8 "…to kill with sword and with hunger and with death and with the beasts of the earth."

Here again is almost identical similarities between two passages that were written around 1,000 years apart. Ezekiel speaks of "noisome beasts" just as Moses recorded in Leviticus that "wild beasts" would come. And I wonder if that might be a reference to wild men, perhaps even terrorists in the employment of the Antichrist.

And notice then the remaining three warnings and how, just as the Leviticus comparison, it lines up perfectly, swords, famines, and death. The Scriptures are simply amazing to study and should be of great interest when these things are found and should inspire the student of prophecy to further read and study the Bible in greater depth.

So Who Is The Rider On The White Horse?

So now back to the question of who the first rider was on the white horse "*And I saw and behold a white horse: and he that sat on him had a bow: and a crown was given to him: and he went forth conquering and to conquer*" (Revelation 6:2)?

The two Old Testament passages in Ezekiel and Revelation are clearly a list of judgments, with the first of the four judgments being referred to as "beasts". In the passage in Ezekiel 14, verse 21 shows, "*For thus saith the Lord God; How much more when I send my four sore judgments upon Jerusalem, the word, and the famine, and the noisome beast, and the pestilence, to cut off from it man and beast?*" Here Ezekiel clearly groups all four of the judgments mentioned as terrible things.

So if these are terrible things, then how could the first rider in Revelation 6 be the Messiah? After studying these and other passages, the first rider cannot only not be the Messiah but can only be the Antichrist or his representative.

When Will The Four Horsemen Appear?

Another question that might be asked concerning the four horsemen is when these horsemen or judgments appear in the prophetic timeline. When is Revelation 6 in comparison to other events, is it before or after the Rapture, and are there things the believer today could look for as some signs that the end times are approaching?

To do that, a comparison of the four horsemen in Revelation 6 and the Lord's outline of the last days in Matthew 24 will be very beneficial. In Matthew 24, the disciples walk with Jesus as they leave Jerusalem and one of them must have noticed and said something about the Temple they were walking by. Perhaps it was just its sheer size or perhaps some continuing construction from Herod's improvements.[60]

Matthew 24	Revelation 6
vs 5 "For many shall come in my name, saying, I am Christ: and shall deceive many"	vs 2 "…and a crown was given to him and he went forth conquering and to conquer."
vs 6 "And ye shall hear of wars and rumors of wars…"	vs 4 "…and there was given unto him a great sword"
vs 7 "…and there shall be famines…"	vs 5 "…A measure of wheat for a penny and three measures of barley for a penny…"
vs 7 "…and pestilences…"	vs 8 "…to kill with sword and with hunger and with death and with the beasts of the earth."

Now there are different views on Matthew 24. For instance, Lewis Chafer held that this passage referred to the church age.[61] But Chafer, like Matthew Henry, who were both great theologians, formed their views long before some things played out concerning prophecy and it should be considered, that if they had seen things like the formation of the nation of Israel in 1948, that they would have looked at Matthew 24 differently.

In contrast, Dwight Pentecost and other reputable theologians insist that Matthew 24 is not history but a prophecy outline and the first section matches Revelation 6?

And it seems that Matthew 24 is not only prophetic but matches, as we shall discuss later, Revelation 6 and gives insight into it.[62]

---

[60]. Tim LaHaye, *Prophecy Study Bible: King James Version* (Chattanooga, TN: AMG Publishers, 2000), 1039.

[61]. Lewis Sperry Chafer, *The Kingdom in History and Prophecy* (Chicago: Bible Institute Colportage Association, 1936), 167.

[62]. Pentecost, 279.

The two conflicting views are caused in part by faulty interpretation from those who hold to other views besides the Pre-millennial view. The Pre-millennial viewpoint holds that this passage is predictive and is yet-to-be fulfilled. In this view, the Tribulation period will begin soon after the return of Christ to receive the church and return to heaven with it. And this leaves Israel and the Jewish people in center stage and the object of the Lord's attention. So the Pre-millennial view, it seems, correctly places the Four Horsemen from Revelation 6 at the beginning of the Tribulation.

A close comparison of the events listed by Jesus with the events released by the four horsemen in Revelation 6 reveals they are the same events. They are even listed in the same sequence. Jesus identified the arrival of false messiahs (Matthew 24:5). John saw the arrival of a specific false messiah, the one called the Antichrist. This is breaking of the first seal, which releases the rider on the white horse (Revelation 6:1-2). This rider is a false messiah hiding behind the imagery of the Lord Jesus Christ.

Jesus identified wars and rumors of war and said, "You will be hearing of wars and rumors of wars. For nation will rise against nation, and kingdom against kingdom." (Matthew 24:6-7). John saw peace would be removed from the earth, which means world war. This is the breaking of the second seal, which releases the rider on the red horse (Revelation 6:3-4). As a result, men begin to slay one another.

Jesus identified famines in various places, which are most likely the same places where wars have been fought because historically famines are a natural by-product of wars (Matthew 24:7). John saw scarcity of food supplies causing hyper-inflation, which causes famines. This is the breaking of the third seal, which releases the rider on the black horse (Revelation 6:5-6).

Jesus identified earthquakes in various places (Matthew 24:7). John saw a rider on an ashen (pale green) horse released after the fourth seal is broken. The rider's name is death, and Hades follows after him. Hades is the place of departed spirits, which is the grave and hell, which are both located below the surface of the earth.

The release of Hades onto the surface of the earth requires the earth to shake and break open, which is why Jesus described it as earthquakes. The Greek word used there is *seismos*, which means shaking. The earth is going to shake as death and Hades are released. Together they will be given authority over a fourth of the earth to bring death through a variety of ways, including the sword, famine, pestilence, and by the wild animals of the earth (Revelation 6:7-8).

So since Jesus and John are both describing the same events occurring in the same order, and since Jesus called these birth pangs, it can be concluded that the trouble caused by the four riders is also the birth pangs. This is significant because it places these events as early in the Tribulation and some might even say leading up to and into the Tribulation. The thought is that while these riders and events related to their appearing are clearly in the Tribulation, that there may be inklings of those very things or problems as time draws near the Tribulation.

The four riders release such great trouble that people might think the end has come, but Jesus said "the end is not yet." In other words, it is not the end of the tribulation period yet or "Great Tribulation" as Jesus mentions in Matthew 24:21. The tribulation is already taking place in the next verse where Jesus said: "*Then shall they deliver you up unto tribulation, and shall kill you and ye shall be hated of all the nations for my name's sake. And then shall many stumble, and shall deliver up one another, and shall hate one another*" (Matthew 24:9-10).

When Do The Four Horsemen Appear?

As to where to place the appearance of the four horsemen, bracketing again will work, which means that since we know what comes before the event and after the event, it is possible to place the event in a timeline. So since the first horseman is the Antichrist and the Antichrist cannot appear until after the Rapture, the four horsemen can only appear after the Tribulation starts.

And as they are the first four seals of a long list of judgments, their appearance is pushed near the beginning of the Tribulation. There are three more seal judgments, which opens seven trumpet judgments, which then opens seven vial judgments.

And since the first rider is the Antichrist, he must appear at the beginning of the Tribulation as he has to sign a seven year peace treaty with Israel and since the Tribulation is only seven years long, he obviously must be present at the beginning to sign it, as other events require it to be signed for them to happen. An example would be the Antichrist breaking the treaty with the Jews at the mid-point of the Tribulation.

So they must appear no later than immediately after the Rapture and may even begin to show up slightly before it!

Chapter 12
The Rise of the Antichrist

The Antichrist has many names in the Scriptures. He is called the "Wicked One", the "Lawless One", the "Beast" and of course, the "Antichrist". Depending on whether a name is defined as a title or just descriptive, the Antichrist has several dozen names in Scripture.[63]

All these names can sometimes confuse readers, especially because the word *Antichrist* is not used in Revelation and is found only in the epistles of 1 John and 2 John. Now, it is not that the Antichrist is not talked about throughout the Scriptures but only in the epistles of John is the word Antichrist used. The name used in the book of Revelation is "The Beast", which has led some to assume that the Beast and the Antichrist are two different characters. And it is this question that we'll look at to see if other prophetic passages can show with certainty that the beast of the book of Revelation and the Antichrist of 1-2 John are one in the same.

But before that, let's take a look at the many names and characteristics about the Antichrist that seem to refer to the one who comes and opposes God and leads the earth to fight against Christ during the Tribulation and some things the Scriptures tell about him will be helpful.

The Many Names of the Antichrist in the Scriptures

The first mention of him may be in Psalm 5:6, where he is called *The Bloody and Deceitful Man* "*Thou shalt destroy them that speak leasing: the Lord will abhor the bloody and deceitful man*". He is called the *Wicked One* "*For the wicked boasteth of his heart's desire and blesseth the covetous, whom the Lord abhoreth. The wicked, through the pride of his countenance, will not seek after God…*" (Psalm 10:3-4). He is called the *Man of the Earth* "*that the man of the earth may no more oppress*" (Psalm 10:18). He is called a *Mighty Man* "*Why boasteth thou thyself in mischief, O mighty man? the good of God endureth…*" (Psalm

---

[63]. Pentecost, 232.

52:1). He is referred to as the *Adversary* "*O God, how long shall the adversary reproach…*" (Psalm 74:10). He is *The Violent M*an "*Deliver me, O Lord from the evil man, preserve me from the violent man*" (Psalm 140:1). He is called *The Spoiler* "*…be thou a covert to them from the face of the spoiler, for the extortioner is at an end, spoiler ceaseth…*" (Isaiah 16:4). He is known as *The Profane and Wicked Prince* "*And thou, profane wicked prince of Israel, whose day is come, when iniquity shall have an end…*" (Ezekiel 21:25). He is called the *Little Horn* "*I considered the horns and behold, there came up among them another little horn, before whom there were three of the first horns plucked up by the roots and behold, in this horn were eyes like the eyes of a man, and a mouth speaking great things*" (Daniel 7:8). He is also called *The Prince that Shall come* "*the prince that shall come shall destroy the city and the sanctuary…*" (Daniel 9:26). He is *The Vile Person* "*And in his estate shall stand up a vile person…and obtain the kingdom by flatteries*" (Daniel 11:21). He is known also in Daniel as *The Willful King* "*And the king shall do according to his will and he shall exalt himself…*" (Daniel 11:36).

    In the New Testament, He is called the *Man of Sin* and *Son of Perdition* "*Let no man deceive you by any means: for that day shall not come, except there come a falling away first, and that man of sin be revealed, son of perdition*" (2 Thessalonians 2:3). Later in that same passage, He is called *The Lawless One* "*Even him, whose coming is after the working of satan with all power and signs and lying wonders*" (2 Thessalonians 2:9).

    And it is finally later in John's epistles that he is called the *Antichrist* "*Who is a liar but he that denieth that Jesus is the Christ? He is antichrist, that denieth the Father and the Son*" (1 John 2:22). And then in the last book of the Bible, he is referred to as the *Beast*[64] "*And when they shall have finished their testimony, the beast that ascendeth out of the bottomless pit shall make war against them and shall overcome them and kill them*" (Revelation 11:7).

---

[64]. John Phillips, *Exploring Revelation*, John Phillips Commentary Series (Grand Rapids: Kregel, 2001), 148.

Characteristics of the Antichrist

Description	Little Horn Daniel 7	Small Horn Daniel 8	Willful King Daniel 11	Man of Lawlessness 2 Thess. 2
Braggart / Egotist	✓	✓	✓	✓
Blasphemer of God	✓	✓	✓	✓
Contemptuous	✓	✓	✓	✓
Persecutor of Believers	✓	✓		
Insolent		✓		
Deceptive / Shrewd		✓		
Demonic		✓		✓
Destructive		✓		✓
Willful		✓	✓	
Sexually Perverted			✓	
Militarist			✓	
Materialist			✓	

Things about the Antichrist from Four Main Passages

What Does the Bible Say about the Antichrist?

Throughout the centuries, Christians have studied these passages on the Antichrist, trying to piece together the what, the where, and who these passages refer to. Not that anyone has to know this to be saved or to live a righteous life, but because every generation is interested in whether the Antichrist will come on the scene in their lifetime.

Polycarp thought it was Caesar in the 2nd century and King Charlemagne of France thought it was Mohammed in 750A.D and Martin Luther thought it was the Pope in the 14th century and Billy Graham, the great evangelist of the twentieth century considered that it was the leader of Soviet communism in his day.[65]

---

[65]. Billy Graham, "Do You Think the Antichrist Is Already Alive? Or Is the Antichrist Just a Symbol or a Figure of Speech?," Billy Graham Evangelistic Association, ttps://billygraham.org/answer/do-you-think-the-antichrist-is-already-alive-or-is-the-

He could be called 'Satan's man' as the overriding purpose of the seven year Tribulation is to bring things to a conclusion and force mankind to choose between Christ and the satan's alternative, the Antichrist. You see, as soon as the rapture happens and Bible believing churches are gone, satan has a clear playing field to set his man up as an alternative messiah. He has been allowed to somewhat rule spiritually over the earth for millenniums but God has restrained him until now from ruling over it politically. It seems that satan has been allowed somewhat of a free hand with the heathen but has been kept back to some degree from those that believed in God.

But after the church has been taken to heaven, the Bible says in 2 Thessalonians 2:8-9 that he will be revealed. And as Daniel said in chapter 7, he will rise as a leader from an old empire, called the fourth beast, that comes to life again. Remember that Daniel is to the Old Testament what Revelation is to the New Testament and so the preponderance of information we have about him is from these two books. And while Revelation sort of gives us a play by play call of what's going on in the Tribulation, it is Daniel who describes him best.

The Antichrist Described In The Book Of Daniel

He is said to be an intellectual genius *"In the latter time of their kingdom, when the transgressors are come to the full, a king fierce countenance and understanding dark sentences shall stand up"* (Daniel 8:23). He will have great oratorical skills *"And the king shall do according to his will and he shall exalt himself and magnify himself above every god and shall speak marvelous things against the God of gods"* (Daniel 11:36).

The Antichrist will be the world's greatest politician as Daniel states that he shall rise from a small nation and quickly take over the nations around him and continue to rise to power until the earth looks to him as their leader.[66] His exploits are covered in Daniel, specifically his political skills in making a

---

antichrist-just-a-symbol-or-a-figure-of-speech/ (accessed October 7, 2017).

[66]. Pink, 53.

treaty with Israel "*And he shall confirm the covenant with many for one week…*" (Daniel 9:27).

The world will love him because he will seem to help the world commercially "*…he shall have power over the treasures of gold and of silver and over all the precious things of Egypt and the Libyans and the Ethiopians shall be at his steps*" (Daniel 11:43). The Antichrist will also seem to be a military genius to his followers as Daniel 11 seems to play out.

He will seem to get his way about everything and his selfishness has no boundaries "*And the king shall do according to his will*" (Daniel 11:36). Scripture also gives some insight into his personal life as it tells that he evidently abandons the religion of his parents or family "*Neither shall he regard the God of his fathers…*" (Daniel 11:37a). And there is a strange phrase that says something about that he does not care for woman, some taking that as saying that he is a homosexual "*…nor the desire of women…*" (Daniel 11:37b).

And the Antichrist just plainly seems to think that he is a god to worshipped "*…nor regard any god for he shall magnify himself above all*" (Daniel 11:37c).

Will Some Be Deceived by the Antichrist and Think He Is the Messiah?

Satan is certainly the master-counterfeiter and his placing and bringing the Antichrist to the forefront of humanity to deceive mankind will be his greatest move. And so it seems that satan goes to great lengths to attempt to disguise the Antichrist, and that many will be taken in when he comes on the scene. In fact, there are several passages that warn of this very thing.

The Lord Himself gave a warning in Matthew 24 as He seems to lay out an outline of the End Times and the Apostle Paul talked of this in 2 Thessalonians 2 as he shares information about what the Tribulation will be like. Both these passages warn of being deceived by "many" or "one" who claims to be Christ and exalts himself as God. And Jesus goes on to say "*For there shall arise false Christs, and false prophets, and shall shew great signs and wonders, insomuch that if it were possible, they shall deceive the very elect*" (Matthew 24:24)

Matthew 24	2 Thessalonians 2
vs 4 "Take heed that <u>no man deceive you</u>"	vs 3 "<u>Let no man deceive you</u> by any means…"
vs 5 "For many shall come in my name, saying, I am Christ, and shall deceive many"	vs 4 "Who opposeth and exalteth himself above all that is called God or that is worshipped, so that he as God sitteth in the temple of God, shewing himself that he is God".

As stated, both of these passages have warnings for God's people to not be deceived and to look for that deceiver to be someone who is claiming to either be the Messiah or God Himself. But why are so many deceived? This next section will look at how satan tries to counterfeit the Antichrist to seem like the real Son of God and since all the Christians from the church age will be gone, the only people initially around in the Tribulation will be the unsaved who are easily led astray.

How Will the Antichrist Mimic the Real Christ?

Christ was revealed at an appointed time as Galatians 4:4 says *"when the fullness of time was come…"*. But notice what 2 Thessalonians 2:6 says *"And now we know what withholdeth that he might be revealed in his time"*. How interesting that satan will bring up his man, the son of perdition, in his time. But instead of God's man coming to save the world, satan's man comes to try to destroy the world.[67] But that is not the only similarity.

Just as Christ was born in the flesh and could be seen, talked to and be around, so will the Antichrist be a real man. Jesus said that if one had seen Him, one had seen the Father and the Antichrist could say that if one had seen him, one had been with the devil. And just as Christ's humanity was shared with his divinity, so will the Antichrist's humanity be shared with the

---

[67]. John F. Walvoord, *The Revelation of Jesus Christ* (Chicago: Moody, 1989), 200.

demonic world. Christ was the God-man and the Antichrist will be a super-demonic-man.

Jesus came as the Messiah, born of the Jewish line as Romans 1:3 states "Concerning His son Jesus Christ our Lord, which was made of the seed of David according to the flesh". And it seems that many think the Antichrist may also be Jewish or part Jewish. One reason people think that is if he was as least part Jewish, it would help him sign a peace treaty with Israel, even though he is from a Gentile nation. Another reason why some think he might be at least part Jewish is his fascination with the Jewish Temple and his desire to want to be worshipped there as he is fixated on Jerusalem.

Others look at the passage where it says *"Neither shall he regard the god of his fathers"* (Daniel 11:37) as stating that he abandon his ancestral religion. And some would suggest that this means that he was likely Jewish but now doesn't practice it. On this point, this writer agrees as it seems it would seem immaterial to a Jew to point out that the enemy of Israel left the worship of some foreign god, for who would care. But as Daniel writes to Jews, they would take note if the Antichrist has left the Jewish faith.

On the topic of whether the Antichrist will be a Jew, David Reagan, who was one of the editors of the Tim LaHaye Prophecy Bible and has his own prophecy television ministry, interviewed twelve prophecy speakers and in general, they all think the Antichrist will either be Jewish or have some partial Jewish heritage.[68] Only Ed Hindson, of Liberty University, thought he would not be Jewish, but Ed Hindson seems to be concentrating on the fact that the Antichrist will be from a Gentile nation and did not consider that he could be from a Gentile nation and still be Jewish or of some Jewish heritage.

Another interesting comparison is that though most who study prophecy know about the "covenant" or treaty that the Antichrist makes with Israel during the Tribulation as was already mentioned in Daniel 9. But the Bible also states that Christ offers Israel a covenant "*…Behold the days come, saith the Lord, when I will make a new covenant with the house of*

---

[68]. Pentecost, 332-336.

Israel, and with the house of Jacob" (Hebrews 8:8), which of course, is based on the passage from the prophet Jeremiah in chapter 31.[69]

Readers of the Scriptures also know that Christ is the believer's High Priest as the book of Hebrews lays out, but a passage in Ezekiel shows that one day, a wicked man shall be removed from being the High Priest *"Thus saith the Lord God: Remove the diadem and take off the crown: this shall not be the same: exalt him that is low and abase him that is high"* (Ezekiel 21:26).

Christ was and will be the King of the Jews, as He not only is God's Son but the literal descendent of King David, who God promised that one day, the Messiah would come from his line and sit and his throne. The Antichrist is flatly called *"The King"* in Daniel 11:36 and just as Christ is called the King of Kings *"…for He is the King of Kings"* (Revelation 17:14), readers are told that many kings will give their power to the Antichrist, making him a 'king of kings' *"And the ten horns which thou sawest are ten kings, which have received no kingdom as yet but receive power as kings one hour with the beast. These have one mind, and shall give their power and strength unto the beast"* (Revelation 17:12-13).

The Lord Jesus was also a miracle worker, healing, calming the storm, walking on water, cursing the fig tree, and many other great things. Christ did these miracles to validate that He was from God for the Jews and that is why Acts 2:22 states *"approved of God among you by miracles and wonders and signs"*. But the prophecies also tell about the Antichrist and that he will either perform some miracles or at least seem to *"Even him, whose coming is after the working of satan with all power and signs and lying wonders"* (2 Thessalonians 2:9). Dwight Pentecost states about this verse that "his claim to power and to deity is proved by signs wrought through satanic power".[70]

Another similarity that the Antichrist would not like is that Christ's public ministry was limited to three and a half years and so will the Antichrist's. Of course Christ's ministry was from

---

[69]. LaHaye, *Prophecy Study Bible*, 791.

[70]. Pentecost, 333.

God and to save the souls of man in contrast to the Antichrist's ministry being from satan and trying to condemn the souls of men. The Tribulation is a full seven years and the Antichrist does begin his rise to power at the start of the Tribulation but he doesn't have full power until after he turns on Israel and that is at the half way point of the Tribulation "*And there was given unto him a mouth speaking great things and blasphemies and power was given unto him to continue forty and two months*" (Revelation 13:5). Isn't it interesting how God really controls things, even the time that the Antichrist is in charge?

When the Lord returns, Scripture says that He will be riding a white horse "*And I saw heaven opened and behold a white horse and He that sat upon Him was called Faithful and True…* (Revelation 19:11), but as has already been discussed, the Antichrist is pictured riding the white horse of a conqueror "*And I saw and behold a white horse: and he that sat on him had a bow and a crown was given unto him and he went forth conquering and to conquer*" (Revelation 6:2).

The last similarity that we will discuss is that just as Christ died and rose again, so the Antichrist may mimic this. Now not everyone interprets Revelation 13 this way, where it says in verse 3 "*And I saw one of his heads as it were wounded to death and deadly wound was healed and all the world wondered after the beast*". So one theory is that perhaps there is an assassination attempt on the Antichrist, and he either is killed or seems to be and that he miraculously comes back to life, or as some think, possessed by satan himself and seems to be alive.[71]

Now not everyone agrees. David Reagan and Ed Hindson, both well respected prophecy speakers think the wound is not to the Antichrist himself but to some aspect of his empire, perhaps to a particular nation. But when we think about that, if a nation was healed it would not seem that people would think it was a miracle. So that does not seem to fit, especially when it does seem that the Antichrist and satan are trying very hard to mimic

---

[71]. Nathan Jones, "Will the Antichrist Be Killed and Resurrected?," The Christ in Prophecy Journal, http://christinprophecyblog.org/2009/06/will-antichrist-be-killed-and/ (accessed October 12, 2017).

Christ and paint the Antichrist as the Messiah. And so to die and rise again would be the ultimate attempt to be like the Messiah.

The Contrasts between Christ and the Antichrist

Obviously, even the titles are in contrast, with one being the Christ and the other the Antichrist, the Lord Jesus being the Man of Sorrows (Isaiah 53:3) and the other the Man of Sin (2 Thessalonians 2:3), Christ being the Son of God (John 1:34) and the other being the Son of Perdition (2 Thessalonians 2:3).

But Christ is called the "*seed of the woman*" (Genesis 3:15) and the Antichrist is called the "*seed of the serpent*" (Genesis 3:15). Christ is called the lamb and the Antichrist is called the beast. Christ is called the Holy One (Mark 1:24) and the Antichrist is called the wicked one (2 Thessalonians 2:8).

Jesus is truth (John 14:6) and the Antichrist is called a lie (John 8:44). Jesus is the Prince of Peace and Ezekiel 21:25 calls the Antichrist a profane prince. Christ is called the "*glorious branch*" (Isaiah 4:2) and the Antichrist is called the "*abominable branch*" (Isaiah 14:19). The Lord is the Good Shepherd while the Antichrist is called an "*idol shepherd*" (Zechariah 11:17).

As far as what they did, there could not be more of a contrast. Christ came down from heaven and the Antichrist came up out of the bottomless pit "*And when they shall have finished their testimony, the beast that ascendeth out of the bottomless pit…*" (Revelation 11:7). Christ came to do His Father's will while the Antichrist came to his own selfish will (Daniel 11:36).

Jesus humbled Himself while the Antichrist exalts himself (Daniel 11:37). Christ honored His fathers (Luke 4:16) while the Antichrist refuses to (Daniel 11:37). Christ ministered to the needy while the Antichrist robs the poor "*…his eyes are privily set against the poor*" (Psalm 10:8). Jesus cleansed the Temple while the Antichrist defiles the Temple (Matthew 24:15). Christ tries to lead the flock (John 10:3) while in contrast, the Antichrist leaves the flock (Zechariah 11:7).

And in the end, their contrasts are even more astounding as Christ was slain for man while the Antichrist slays man. Christ was received up into heaven while the Antichrist goes down into the Lake of Fire "*And the beast was taken and with him the false prophet...These both were cast alive into a lake of fire burning with brimstone*".

Studying the difference between Christ and the Antichrist, not only lifts up Christ as the glorious Messiah but shows the utter despicable nature of the Antichrist.

So Is the Beast of Revelation the Antichrist?

As this writer looks at the many passages that talk about the adversary of Israel throughout the Old Testament, and then find him mentioned again in the New Testament, it seems clear that when the "Antichrist" is mentioned in the epistles of John and when the "Beast" is mentioned in Revelation, that they are one in the same. And so for those who don't think the Beast in Revelation is the Antichrist, who do they think he is? They usually end up with the view that the False Prophet of Revelation is the Antichrist. But as we will see, this just cannot be so.

Reasons The Antichrist And The False Prophet In Revelation Cannot Be One In The Same

In his book, *The Antichrist*, A. W. Pink presents seven points of argument that the "Beast" of Revelation is the same as the Antichrist in the rest of the Scriptures.[72]

His first point is that the Antichrist cannot be the second beast of Revelation, which is often called the 'False Prophet' as the second beast is clearly subservient to the first beast. And if the Antichrist is claiming to be the Messiah for the Jews, he could not be under someone else and still claim to be their king to lead them out of Gentile bondage.

Secondly, if the Antichrist is trying to mimic Christ, then it is the first beast of Revelation that is setting up a kingdom, not the second beast, for the second beast's efforts are in the arena of religion, bringing all religions to worship the first beast.

Thirdly, the beast and the false prophet cannot be the same person for they are individually judged and both cast into the Lake of Fire "*And the beast was taken and with him the false*

---

[72]. Pink, 89.

prophet…These both were cast alive into a lake of fire burning with brimstone" (Revelation 19:20).

Fourthly, the description of the "beast" from Revelation lines up with many other prophecies about the Antichrist from the rest of Scripture as we have pointed out in length.

Fifthly, the second beast, which must be the false prophet, causes the earth to worship the first beast, which is of course, a desire of the Antichrist, that is to be worshipped "*And I beheld another beast coming up out of the earth…And he exerciseth all the power of the first beast…and causeth the earth and them which dwell therein to worship the first beast whose deadly wound was healed*" (Revelation 13:11-12).

Sixthly, the concept that there is an unholy trinity seems striking and convincingly a desire of satan. For him to have a messiah in the Antichrist, a religious persuader in the false prophet, and then for satan himself to be god, fits what is known of his ultimate desire to be like the most high.

And lastly, the book of Daniel and Revelation line up too many things that parallel the Antichrist and the beast.

The Unholy Trinity as found in the book of Revelation

A Comparison of the Antichrist in the Epistles of John and the Beast of Revelation 13

It is important before looking at these passages to remember that the epistles of John were not necessarily intended to be prophetic passages concerning the rise of the Antichrist but was the beloved John the Apostle writing in love to encourage those he knew to follow the Lord. But though details about the Antichrist were not the primary point of the epistles, John's epistles still show the similarity between the Antichrist of the epistles and the beast of the revelation.

Epistles of 1 and 2 John	Revelation 13
1 John 2:18 "antichrist shall come…it is the last time"	vs 1 "…I stood upon the sand of the sea and saw a beast rise up…"
1 John 2:22 "Who is a liar but he that denieth that Jesus is Christ? He is an antichrist"	vs 1 "…and upon his heads the name of blasphemy".
1 John 4:3 "Every spirit that confesseth not that Jesus Christ is come in the flesh is not of God and this is that spirit of antichrist…"	vs 5 "And there was given unto him a mouth speaking great things and blasphemies.."
2 John 1:7 "For many deceivers are entered into the world, who confess not that Jesus is come in the flesh. This is a deceiver and an antichrist.	vs 8 "And all that dwell upon the earth shall worship him, whose names are not written in the blook of life…"

I think the above comparison clearly shows the similarities between the Antichrist of John's epistles and the Beast of the book of Revelation.

Chapter 13
The 144,000

The number seems mesmerizing! They are one of the most mysterious groups mentioned in the Bible. Many sects and cults have claimed to literally be them. But who are the 144,000 witnesses mentioned in Revelation chapter 7? Are these the only people who make it to Heaven out the Tribulational period? Are these supernatural beings who will descend to Earth in the end times? The answer to both of those questions is no, as the Bible actually does identify the 144,000 and answers questions about who they are and shows that they have a very important role in God restoring the nation of Israel and the world in the final days before the Second Coming of Jesus Christ.

The main passage on the topic is Revelation 7:3-4 *"Saying hurt not the earth neither the sea, nor the trees, till we have sealed the servants of our God in their foreheads. And I heard the number of them which were sealed an hundred and forth and four thousand of all the tribes of the children of Israel"*. Chapter seven describes the midst of God's judgment on the earth during the seven years of tribulation. And yet there is a magnificent level of control by God over all the factors of space and time and events and John Phillips describes this as *"a calm in the midst of a storm"*.[73]

That brief time of setting aside of the terrible judgments is so God can still reach out into mankind, specifically the Jews, and bring them back to Himself. Scripture states that the angel that seals the 144,000 comes from the east *"And I saw another angel ascending from the east…"* (Revelation 7:2) and "seals", which for now is at least the setting aside for service these servants of God to totally defy satan's dominion and the will of the Antichrist.

Chapter seven goes on to specify that the number 144,000 is attained by the angel sealing 12,000 from twelve different tribes of Israel. And this initially brings up the question as to whether there are twelve tribes of Israel still in existence to which the answer evidently is yes and that God evidently knows exactly

---

[73]. Phillips, *Exploring Revelation*, 109.

who and where they are. They were scattered during the many dispersions throughout the centuries but it is not as if they disappeared and can somewhat be traced to different areas of the world and often even found in communities.[74]

This section of Revelation regarding the 144,000 Jews being "sealed" is perhaps one of the most abused passages in prophetic Scripture. For instance, the Jehovah Witnesses claim that their founders and early followers constituted this group and many other cults have claimed to be them through the ages. And then others have claimed that this passage is not literal but purely symbolic of the church.

Regarding whether the 144,000 are symbolic, there are just too many purposeful details regarding them and it is clear that the passage must be taken literally. Some details of the passage are:

Earthly Conditions Are Set Aside for This to Take Place (7:1)

Symbolism has no concern as to the weather, the wind, the waves, or trees nor any other condition as if it is symbolic, it would not matter. And yet, verse one says "And after these things I saw four angels standing on the four corners of the earth, holding the four winds of the earth, that the wind should not blow on the earth, nor the sea, nor on any tree". So with these concerns the danger to them must be real and thus the passage must be literal.

The Number of Angels Is Very Specific, Even Differentiating (7:1-2)

Passages using symbolism are not usually concerned with peripheral details or numbers. And yet verse one states that there are *"four angels standing on the four corners of the earth"* and then verse 2 states that John saw *"another angel"*. If this passage was symbolic, what would it matter to state that there was a different angel that was not part of the first group. A detail like

---

[74]. "Where Are the Ten Lost Tribes of Israel?," https://www.geni.com/projects/Where-are-The-Ten-Lost-Tribes-of-Israel/3474 (accessed October 20, 2017).

this shows that John as an eye witness sees this literally happening.

Directional Statements Are Given (7:2)

If the 144,000 represent some past group, such as the church or some sub-set of Christianity, then why would readers need to know from what direction the angel came. And yet, notice *"And I saw another angel ascending from the east…"*. Not only are readers told from what direction but that the angel was coming down, both details that have no meaning or significance if this group is just an illustration.

The Angels Are Interactive (7:2-3)

Frankly, there are very few passages where angels are interactive, for example the ones in the Gospels where angels conversed with Joseph and Mary regarding the birth of Christ and then appearing to the shepherds were interactive. And so if these angels were real, then why should not the angels in this passage be real as well. And notice that the angel that came from the east interacts with the other angels. In verse 2 the angel *"cried with a loud voice"* and in verse 3, the angel is *"saying"*.

Why Mention "Foreheads"? (7:3)

Having read several viewpoints that look at the 144,000 as symbolic, none present any reason that the foreheads are mentioned. That is not even a Jewish 'thing' as the Jews refer to 'bowels' and 'heart' and even 'mind' but there is nothing in Hebrew culture that would explain why their "foreheads" are sealed. It is common knowledge that in symbolic literature that the presence of unnecessary details that are often proof that the passage is to be taken literally.[75]

Imagine a made up story that has the intent of making a point and there would likely not be unnecessary details but then think of someone telling a story that was real, that the teller had

---

[75]. Pentecost, 13.

seen, and there would be details and facts that are just seemingly extra, although true.

The Number Is So Very Specific (7:4)

The author could have said 'thousands' or 'multitudes' or even 'a number beyond measure' or even 'a great host' but the number was a specific 144,000 *"And I heard the number of them which were sealed and there were sealed an hundred and forty and four thousand…"*..

As mentioned above, the details of the passage lend the reader to a literal understanding and interpretation. And the size of the number is significant and meaningful too.

Why not 'twelve' as in the disciples or why not 'one hundred and twenty' as in the gathering in the upper room? Why not 'four hundred' or 'seven hundred' or even 'one thousand'. But the author evidently states that number before him, the astounding and evidently impressive 144,000. It is a number so large and so specific that it cannot be taken any other way than literally.

The Breakdown of the Number (7:5-8)

Another overwhelming aspect of this passage is that not only is the total number of 144,000 given but then the passage breaks down how 12,000 come from each of the twelve tribes listed. There is no possible allegorical position here for how would the church age, which some think this represents, possibly know what each tribe is intended to be.

The Absence of Two Tribes (7:5-8)

A careful listing of the twelve tribes of Israel mentioned in this passage will have the reader noticing a few irregularities. The original twelve sons of Jacob included both Levi and Joseph but at Jacob's death, he blessed two of Joseph's sons, Ephraim and Manasseh, who Jacob elevated to the place of his sons, to sort of repay Joseph for what his brothers had done to him. And when Levi was designated the priestly tribe, that still made it twelve tribes plus the Levitical tribe.

But when John lists the tribes from which the 144,000 were being sealed, the tribes of Dan and Ephraim are missing. A reasonable explanation for this is that both Dan and Ephraim were responsible at different times for leading the children of Israel into idolatry.

Perhaps this is what the Lord was thinking of when he wrote *"Lest there should be among you…to go and serve the gods of these nations…And the Lord shall separate him unto evil out of all the tribes of Israel…"* (Deuteronomy 29:18-21).

And when Jeroboam became king of the ten tribes that rebelled against Solomon's son Rehoboam, in order to keep his people from going to Jerusalem to worship, he set up false centers of worship in both Ephraim and Dan *"Whereupon the king took counsel and made two calves of gold…and he set the one in Bethel (Ephraim) and the other put he in Dan"* (1 Kings 12:28-29).

So it appears that the two tribes that either were responsible for idolatry or permitted it the most will not be entrusted with sharing the truth during the Tribulation.

The Details of the Witnesses (14:4-5)

The 144,000 are mentioned later in the book of Revelation, where some additional details are given and it is the nature of these details that would also lend towards a literal interpretation of the passage. In speaking of the witnesses *"These are they which were not defiled with women; for they are virgins. These are they which follow the Lamb whithersoever He goeth. These were redeemed from among men, being the first-fruits unto God and to the Lamb. And in their mouth was found no guile for they are without fault before the throne of God"*. And so that brings the question…

Are the 144,000 of Revelation 7 the Same As the 144,000 in Revelation 14?

Chapter seven gives that initial number and that they are sealed and the twelve tribes that they are called out of. But then in Revelation fourteen, a group of people numbering 144,000 again is brought up. But being further along in the seven years of the Tribulation, much has evidently transpired and these witnesses appear on Mount Zion with the Lord, singing a song and praising God.

So a logical question would be that if they are not the same, why would God have another group of exactly the same number and not think that readers would need an explanation of who they were. In the book of Revelation, the Apostle John actually either asks or is being told who everyone is. It would be strange for another group of people, so large and yet so distinct to appear with no explanation if they were not the same group mentioned in Revelation 7. So assuming they are the same group, let's see if there are some similarities between the two groups.

Revelation 7	Revelation 14
Vs 4 "…an hundred and forty and four thousand"	Vs 3 "…but the hundred and forty and four thousand…"
Vs 2 "…till we have sealed the servants of our God in their foreheads"	Vs 1 "…having his Father's name written in their foreheads"
Vs 2 "And I saw another angel…"	Vs 6 "And I saw another angel…"

So not only is the number the same but notice that they both belong to God, the "sealed" likely being the "Father's name". And that they both have this in their "foreheads" is just too much of a coincidence. And of course, they are both in a time and place that angelic activity is all around them.

There are those that think the group is different, such as Tim LaHaye who think this is a group of Gentiles Christians who have faithfully served the Lord.[76] LaHaye admits that he would like to see them as the same group but is concerned that the vision that sees the Lord on Mount Zion in chapter fourteen does

---

[76]. Tim LaHaye, *Revelation: Illustrated and Made Plain* (Grand Rapids: Zondervan, 1974), 89.

not fit the Pre-tribulational timeline. It seems that LaHaye considers that though Revelation is to be taken literally, not everything is exactly chronological, as the scenes do rotate between heaven and earth.

In fact, some think that Revelation fourteen is a flash forward to the end of the Tribulation, which gives the reader a preview of what lies ahead, because it assures the ultimate triumph to the Lord Jesus.[77] But another view is that Revelation fourteen is looking into heaven itself, which if so, would not affect a Pre-tribulational timeline as it places Christ in heaven during the Tribulation and then the 144,000 have either been martyred or raptured into heaven to be with the Lord.[78]

And for those who would argue that their sealing and protection must mean that they could not be martyred, I would remind them that God seals or protects for a time period and from His perspective, when the task or time period is over, it is perfectly normal for His servants to be translated to heaven, even if that is by the means of death. The Apostle Paul was sealed as a apostle to the Gentiles and yet when his task was done or race was ran, he was martyred. And even in the case of the two witnesses that preach against the Antichrist, which we will discuss later, when their time was done, they were killed. So it would not be abnormal for God to seal 144,000 evangelists and then when their job was done, allow them to taste death.

So Why Are They Virgins?

"*These are they which were not defiled with women, for they are virgins…*" (Revelation 14:4). There may be a simple practical reason, that being that if these witnesses are to take off all over the world, being single with no family to worry about would sure free them up. Along this line of thinking, is that if they are unmarried and do not even have a girlfriend, then there would be no worries about the Antichrist trying to retaliate against them and someone they loved.

---

[77]. Walvoord, 145.

[78]. Phillips, *Exploring Revelation*, 179.

And though there is likely merit in the above thoughts, there is something in the Scriptures about those who have not had sexual relations and are completely pure, like the Lord Jesus was. Jesus even spoke of this when the Pharisees came to ask Christ in an attempt to trick Him, in asking about whose wife would someone be in heaven if she was married to more than one man on earth. After Jesus answered, saying that the bonds of marriage did not exist in heaven, Jesus' disciples asked if it was better just to not be married here on earth *"His disciples say unto Him, If the case of the man be with his wife, it is not good to marry"* (Matthew 19:10).

The Lord responded by saying that there are some that remain unmarried and that they did so for the kingdom's sake, meaning that there are some who remain not only single but celibate for the reason that in doing so, they not only stay pure but can focus singularly on serving God. *"But He said unto them, All men cannot receive this saying, save they to whom it is given. For there are some eunuchs, which were so born from their mother's womb and there are some eunuchs which were made eunuchs of men and there be eunuchs which have made themselves eunuchs for the kingdom of heaven's sake. He that is able to receive it, let him receive it"* (Matthew 19:11-12)

What Are the 144,000 Doing in God's Plan?

Though one may assume they preach and witness for the Lord Jesus, all the text actually says is that they are "servants" in Revelation 7:3. It can be assumed that they are preachers or evangelists because of what comes next in the passage *"After this I beheld and lo a great multitude which no man could number of all nations and kindreds and people and tongues stood before the throne and before the Lamb, clothed with white robes and palms in their hands"* (Revelation 7:9). The order seems to insinuate that the great multitude was saved in connection to the witness of the 144,000. [79]

Another purpose they may have is to be the harbingers of truth in a time where satan and his Antichrist are doing nothing

---

[79]. LaHaye, *Prophecy Study Bible*, 1375.

but lying. And just as Elijah was "*he who troubleth Israel*" to King Ahab, so these 144,000 are a thorn in the Beast's side. They will be a constant reminder that though millions will bow to his will, that God still will let him go no further than God allows. And neither the armies of the Antichrist, nor the spies of the false prophet, nor even satan himself can touch these sealed of God.

Perhaps it is that God always leaves a witness or always has a remnant or loves man enough to make sure the plan of salvation is still presented even during the Tribulation or that God wants the earth to see that the Antichrist does not rule over everything but whatever the reason or reasons, the 144,000 fulfill it and evidently, many are saved!

The twelve tribes from whom the 144,000 are called from. Notice that Dan and Ephraim are missing

Chapter 14
The Invasion of Gog and Magog

The mention of Gog and Magog brings up images of a great battle during the end times. Gog and Magog appear in the book of Ezekiel. Some think they are referred to in the book of Revelation and the prophesied invasion of Israel or at least in the Middle East and the event is normally placed during the Seven Years of Tribulation.

Now not everyone agrees on all the details. For instance, Dwight Pentecost identifies them as just part of the northern confederacy and actually has them fighting against the Antichrist's revived Roman empire.[80] John Walvoord seems to sort of set them apart in their political and then military ambitions and though there are other nations against Israel, he seems to think that they are acting independently.[81] And Mark Hitchcock who comments in the Ryrie Study Bible says on this topic that Gog and Magog represent perhaps all the nations in the end times that are against Israel.[82]

The setting in Ezekiel is that God has just regathered Israel in the end times "I shall put my spirit in you and ye shall live and I shall place you in your own land…"(Ezekiel 37:14) and "…Thus saith the Lord God; Behold, I will take the children of Israel from among the heathen whither they be gone and will gather them into their own land" (Ezekiel 37:21). And so it seems to be this that begins to bother the heathen nations, specifically the nations to the north that are known in the Bible as Gog and Magog.

So Who Is Gog and Magog?

Josephus, the Jewish Historian, wrote concerning them that they were the descendents of Japheth the son of Noah.[83] And

---

[80]. Pentecost, 327.

[81]. Walvoord, 303.

[82]. Ryrie, 876.

[83]. Flavius Josephus, "The Antiquities of the Jews," Documenta Catholica Omnia, http://www.documentacatholicaomnia.eu/03d/0037-

there are ancient maps that do show Gog and Magog to the north just like the Bible says.

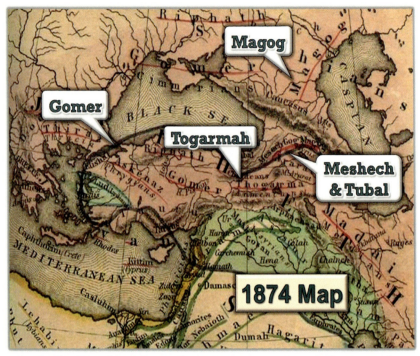

Ezekiel's War has always been interesting in prophetic studies

    In the Scriptures, Gog seems to be the leader and is also called the prince of Meshech and Tubal and most seem to identify this with the modern day country of Russia, which would line up with the armies of Gog and Magog coming from the north as Russia is directly north of Israel.

    In the Scriptural account of this war, there are others involved as between Ezekiel thirty-eight and thirty-nine, there is a list of countries involved: Rosh, Magog, Meshech, Tubal, Persia, Cush, Gomer and Beth-Togarmah. And it seems clear that their purpose is to invade Israel to loot and plunder *"To take spoil and to take a prey to turn thine hand upon the desolate places that are now inhabited and upon the people that are gathered out*

0103,_Flavius_Josephus,_The_Antiquities_Of_The_Jews,_EN.pdf (accessed October 30, 2017).

of the nations, which have gotten cattle and goods, that dwell in the midst of the land" (Ezekiel 38:12).

But it seems that this was all the Lord's plan as were told "*…and I will bring thee forth and all thine army, horses and horsemen…*" (Ezekiel 38:4) just so the Lord could defeat them "And I will turn thee back and leave but the sixth part of thee" (Ezekiel 39:2) and "*Thou shalt fall upon the mountains of Israel, thou, and all thy bands, and the people that is with thee…*" (Ezekiel 39:4).

So the end result is that even though Gog and Magog were attacking a seemingly defenseless Israel, it was God that pulled them out of their lands to the north "*and put hooks into thy jaws and I will bring thee forth*" (Ezekiel 38:4) only to destroy them on the mountains of Israel.

The purpose of this, besides bringing about end time justice, was for God to show His glory to the nations of the earth and to Israel itself "*Thus will I magnify myself and sanctify myself and I will be known in the eyes of many nations and they will know that I am God*" (Ezekiel 38:23).[84] And so the Lord uses this great supernatural victory to make not only His presence real but His involvement in the world's affairs plain to see. And perhaps this event is what brings Israel to belief during the Tribulation.

So Who Is Gog and Magog?

One way to determine who Gog and Magog are, would be to figure out who the leader is, as that study not only uses the reference to Gog but goes further in details, naming what he is prince over. The leader of this alliance or northern confederation is called …"*the chief prince of Meshech and Tubal*" (Ezekiel 38:2). Some, like David Richardson, who think the last kingdom of the prophecy of Daniel is a Middle East confederation and not the old Roman empire, think the chief of Gog is none other than the Antichrist. His reasoning is that since he believes that the Antichrist will be from the Middle East, that there cannot be another invader from the north from outside of the Middle East and that with his interpretation, after the northern confederation is

---

[84]. Pentecost, 508–509.

defeated, which he says are the armies of the Antichrist, that peace comes to Israel and for that to happen, the battle has to be the battle of Armageddon. [85] Though I respect the work that Richardson has put into the possible view of the last world empire being the old Ottoman empire, I think he is grouping all these things together unnecessarily.

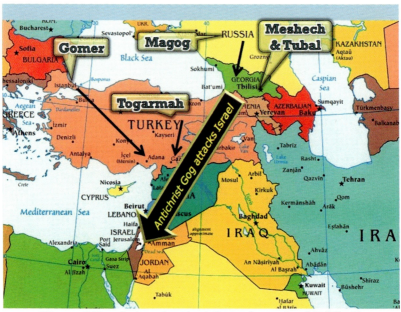

View of Gog being the Antichrist from the Middle East

Others think the Prince of Gog is from past history and was Antiochus Epiphenes from the book of Daniel and that this battle has already taken place. Theologians like Daniel Whedon clearly think this saying "after examining all previous inions... Antiochus Epiphenes...is alone intended here and that Gog...is an allusion to the well-known character of Antiochus, whom historians describe as an artful, cunning, and dissembling man".[86] He and others refer back to the Table of Nations where the world

---

[85]. Joel Richardson, "Six Reasons Why Gog Is the Antichrist/Beast," https://joelstrumpet.com/6-reasons-why-gog-is-the-antichrist-beast/ (accessed October 29, 2017).

[86]. Daniel Whedon, *Daniel Whedon's Commentary on the Old Testament*, (n.p.: Grace Works Media, 2010), 8:79.

was much smaller and "north" was not so far as Russia but just north of Syria into the modern country of Turkey.

Table of nations map from Genesis 10

Others, including Richard Fruchtenbaum, who Tim LaHaye and Thomas Ice quote a lot in their books on the end times, lays out what some would call the traditional view, that being that Gog and Magog are referring to the modern day Russia, although they would counter that Russia is anything but modern day as shall be clear in a moment.[87] He states that no Middle Eastern nation seems to fit the passage and that there is Scripture evidence that the Prince of Meshach is the leader of Russia.

There are several reasons that many lean towards the Prince of Gog being the leader of Russia. One of the most convincing items is that the word for *"Chief Prince"* in Ezekiel 38:2 is actually 'Prince of Rosh'. The word *"chief"* in Hebrew is *Rosh* and many identify this with the descendents of Japheth that settled way north. And since both Meshech and Tubal are sons

---

[87]. Ron Thompson, "The Coming World War: Gog and Magog," https://gpront.wordpress.com/2015/05/11/the-coming-world-war-gog-and-magog/ (accessed October 29, 2017).

of Japheth it would seem that "*Rosh*" would be to the north as part of the Gentiles nations "*The sons of Japheth; Gomer, and Magog, and Madai and Javan and Tubal and Meshech and Tiras*" (Genesis 10:2).

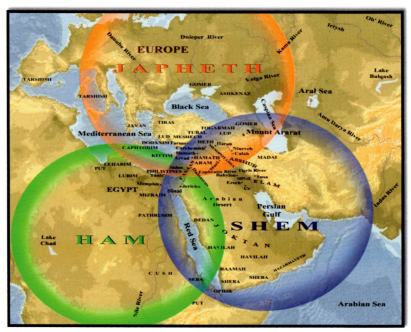

Descendants of Noah

One reason there is perhaps disagreement over who the "*Prince of Rosh*" might be is a translation issue. In looking at Ezekiel 38:3 which first mentions "*the chief prince of Meshech and Tubal*" is that "*Rosh*" is missing as it was translated as "*chief*". But for instance in the New King James Version and other translations, it reads "*the prince of Rosh, Meshech, and Tubal…*". And a word for word translation from an interlinear Bible says "*And against Rosh the prince…*".[88] So if an early biblical commentator is not looking for "*Rosh*", he might not be looking at Russia and look no further than Turkey.

But why the differences in translation? The challenge is simply in interpreting the word "*Rosh*" or "*Ros*". Is it a noun

---

[88]. Jay P. Green, ed., *The Interlinear Bible* (Lafayette, Indiana: Sovereign Grace, 1985), 668.

based on an actual land area or is it an adjective based on the Hebrew word "*Rosh*" which means "*head*", "*top*", or "*chief*". So some translators went with the old Hebrew word for "*chief*" while others thought it was one of the lands that were mentioned in the verse. The King James translators went with the Latin Vulgate using it as an adjective while the New King James translators went with the Greek Septuagint (LXX) and used it as a noun.

Some Reasons Rosh Could Be Talking about Russia

1. Some might claim that it would be unusual for the Bible to reach out into the future and predict a nation's involvement in prophecy that did not exist at the time. But is not that the nature of prophecy? In the book of Daniel, should the word "Grecian" in Daniel "*And now will I she thee the truth. Behold there shall stand up yet three kings in Persia and the fourth shall be far richer than they all and by his strength through his riches he shall stir up all against the realm of Grecia*" (Daniel 11:2) be taken as some sort of misinterpretation because when Greece is mentioned, it did not really exist as a strong nation, let alone an empire. So it is not abnormal for the Scriptures to reach far out into the future and name a nation that might not be known at the time that the prophecy was written.

2. While some scholars do interpret "*Rosh*" as "*chief*", others such as G.A. Cook believe "Rosh" to be a noun form and if it is a noun, then it would be a land like the other lands mentioned like Meshech and Tubal. In his book 'Northern Storm Rising', Ron Rhodes quotes Cook on this very topic: "Exegetically, the evidence supports taking 'Rosh' as a proper noun (that is as a geographical area). G. A. Cook, a Hebrew scholar, says that 'this is the most natural way of rendering the Hebrew.'"[89] And in a passage that list other geographical lands, why could "Rosh" not be another geographical land? For if "*Rosh*" was just the leader, then why are the other leaders of the other countries not listed? It

---

[89]. Ron Rhodes, *Northern Storm Rising: Russia, Iran, and the Emerging End-Times Military Coalition Against Israel* (Eugene, OR: Harvest House, 1995), 106.

would be very consistent to translate "*Rosh*" as one of the lands that was going to rise up against Israel.

3. Of the two sources concerning the translation, the Septuagint (LXX) translation predates the Latin Vulgate by 700 years, which makes the Septuagint only three centuries removed from the time of Ezekiel. The point would be that the Jews translating the Hebrew Bible into Greek would have had a better idea of what "Rosh" meant than the Catholics would 700 years later. This is a heavy point. Too often the time past is read as sort of scooting along without realizing the actual breadth and impact of time. Ponder how much can happen in seven hundred years. Seven hundred years ago, the New World was not even discovered and most of Europe was in the dark ages and the reformation was still two hundred years away. The existence of the Septuagint (LXX) is an unequaled source of insight into many passages of the Old Testament. In research in the Septuagint, Jan Joosten from Oxford says "In researching almost any part of the Old Testament that ventures outside the local area of Israel, the Septuagint is invaluable".[90] To not consider what the Septuagint says is simply irresponsible for anyone trying to interpret ancient Scripture.

4. Many early history references, for example the tenth century Byzantine writers such as Ibn Fadlan, identified a group of Scythians dwelling in the northern parts upon the river Volga as the "Ros". In his writings, he described a people called the "Rusiyyah" as the Volga Vikings who lived on the Volga River, in modern day Russia.

5. Assyrian texts that predate Ezekiel refer to the Rosh or Rashu as those that live north in modern day Russia and that Rosh was a well-known place in antiquity and was easily found in ancient literature.[91] The name for a land of Rosh was also found ten

---

[90]. Jan Joosten, "Textual Criticism and the Septuagint," http://ohb.berkeley.edu/Joosten,%20LXX%20in%20OHB.pdf (accessed December 21, 2017), 17.

[91]. Price, James, "Rosh: An Ancient Land Known to Ezekiel," *Grace Theological Journal* 6, no. 1 (1985): 69.

times in Sargon's inscriptions and five times on some Ugaritic tablets.

6. What better nation fits the description in Ezekiel 39:1-2 where it says "*I will turn thee back and leave but the sixth part of thee and will cause thee to come up from the north parts…*", the "north parts" meaning far north. And Russia easily is from the far north.

Map of end-time nations. Magog - Kazakhstan, Kyrgyzstan, Uzbekistan, Turkmenistan, Tajikistan, Afghanistan; Rosh - Russia; Meshech - Tubal, Gomer, Beth-togarmah, Turkey (and possibly Azerbaijan, Armenia)

7. Modern day Russia, meaning the Russia of the last one hundred years, has sought out alliances with the Islamic nations of the Middle East, often supplying them with economic assistant and military hardware.

With these thoughts, it seems not only possible but likely that the Prince of Rosh is the leader of the modern day nation of Russia.

When Do Gog and Magog Invade?

In a poll given to those at a prophecy conference the question was put to them as to "When Will the God-Magog Battle Happen"? Of the 687 respondents that cast their vote, the results showed a wide range of opinions as to when they thought this battle would occur.[92]

Table 2. When Will the Gog-Magog Battle Happen? (Votes included in this survey - 687)

When will the Gog-Magog Battle happen?	
Before Rapture	101 (14%)
Before Tribulation	245 (35%)
During Tribulation	248 (36%)
End Millennium	47 (6%)
Already Has	7 (1%)
Never	39 (5%)

Votes so far: 687

An interpretation of the poll must take into account that some of those responding may not have any serious reasons for their answer, but even taking the survey with a little skepticism, it does show an overwhelming understanding that the battle takes place either right before the Tribulation or during it. Yes, there were those who may be confusing it for the battle of Armageddon but over 71% place it in or around the Tribulation.

---

[92]. "The Battle of Ezekiel 38-39: Part 2," Grace thru Faith, https://gracethrufaith.com/end-times-prophecy/the-battle-of-ezekiel-38-39-part-2/ (accessed December 21, 2017).

It seems a common consent, other than to Preterists who falsely believe that most prophecy is past, that Gog and Magog are in the end times scenario. But there is some confusion, with some thinking that the account in Ezekiel is the same as the Battle for Armageddon. But it does not seem so when comparing Ezekiel's Gog and Magog battle and the Battle mentioned at the end of the Tribulation accounted for in Revelation 16-19, commonly known as the Battle of Armageddon.

In Tim LaHaye's book, 'Charting the End Time' he states that this battle cannot be the battle of Armageddon as not all nations are fighting for the same cause and he is correct. In the Battle of Armageddon, every nation is against Israel "*…which go forth unto the kings of the earth and of the whole world, to gather them to the battle of that great day of God Almighty…And he gathered them together into a place called in the Hebrew tongue Armageddon*" (Revelation 6:14-16).

Another reason is that in Revelation 16, which describes the Battle of Armageddon, the attack on Israel comes from the whole earth while in Ezekiel 38, the invasion comes from only the northern confederation.[93]

Thirdly, Ezekiel 38 is clear about the reason for the invasion, that being to "take spoil" while the reason for the Battle for Armageddon is to defy the God of heaven "*And I saw the beast and the kings of the earth, and their armies, gathered together to make war against Him (Christ) that sat on the horse and against his army*" (Revelation 19:19).

It also seems that the invasion of Ezekiel 38 is a protest against someone else invading but in the Battle of Armageddon, there is no protest mentioned, no sides or kings of the north facing off against the kings of the south "*And the king of the south shall be moved with choler and shall come forth and fight with him, even with the king of the north: and he shall set forth a great multitude…*" (Daniel 11:11).

And perhaps the best argument that the battle in Ezekiel cannot be the Battle of Armageddon is where and how the invaders in Ezekiel are destroyed in contrast to those who gather at the Battle of Armageddon. Those attacking in Ezekiel are said

---

[93]. LaHaye and Ice, *Charting the End Times*, 93.

to end their campaign on a mountain "*...and is gathered out of many people, against the mountains of Israel, which have always been waste...*" (Ezekiel 38:8) while the battle of Armageddon is in the Valley of Megiddo.

And as far as how they are destroyed, Ezekiel states that the army from the north will be destroyed supernaturally by supernatural disasters "*...surely in that day there shall be a great shaking in the land of Israel. So that the fishes of the sea, and fowls of the heaven and beast of the field and all creeping things that creep upon the earth and all the men that are upon the face of the earth shall shake at my presence and the mountains shall be thrown down and the steep places shall fall...*" (Ezekiel 38:19-20). In contrast, in Revelation, it is the Lord Jesus Himself that comes from heaven and destroys the armies of earth gathered against Him "*And out of His mouth goeth a sharp sword that with it he should smite the nations...*" (Revelation 19:15).

Reasons Why the Invasion of Gog and Magog happen during the First Part of the Tribulation or around the Half way point.

1. Ezekiel 36-38, among other things, is stating that the Jews will be re-gathered in Israel for the Lord's coming. To place this invasion in the past does not fit any known era where the Jews were being re-gathered in Israel, other than the time of 1948-1967. And to this writer's knowledge, no one talks about the War for Independence in 1948 or the Six Day War of 1967 being the war with Gog and Magog.

2. The passage in Ezekiel uses language that purposely places it in the end time. The passage uses "*latter years*" (Ezekiel 38:8) and "last days" (Ezekiel 38:16). To pull this event out and claim that it has already happened would be very inconsistent with other references to the last days and end times. To do this would say that perhaps all of prophecy has already happened

3. That this invading alliance is supernaturally destroyed also does not fit anything that has already happened in history. There have been many invasions of Israel not only in the Old Testament and since then as well. And God has supernaturally intervened a few times as He did with the Assyrians in 2 Kings 18. But all

these happened before the prophecy of Ezekiel and since then, nothing even comes close to seeing the direct intervention of God.

4. The alliance mentioned has never been in place. Ezekiel 38 list very specific nations *"Persia, Ethiopia, and Libya…"* (Ezekiel 38:5) and those nations have never been in alliance with Russia before or for that matter Turkey or Assyria or Iran and in fact, have if anything had a history of being at odds with the aforementioned nations. Now there are some that do not take the listing of nations literally such as the Pulpit Commentary which says "These allied nations are depicted as coming from the four corners of the globe. Persia from the east; Ethiopia or Cush from the south; Libya or Phut from the west; and Gomer, the Cimmerians of Homer, whose abodes were the shores of the Euzine and Caspian Seas, and the Gimirrai of the Assyrian Inscriptions with the house of Tegarmah, from the north, or the extreme regions of the north.".[94] But since prophetic passages liberally and often use phrases that would mean 'from the four corners of the earth' or 'all the nations', it would be inconsistent to think that in this case, it did not mean the actual nations listed.

5. At no time in history has Israel named a valley Hamon Gog (Ezek. 39:11), nor the adjoining town called Hamonah existed where the Jews buried the invaders. History just does not show such a battle has ever happened, which only leaves a future timing for it to occur.

And now after giving reasons that the invasion of Gog and Magog cannot have happened in the past, we will compare the passage in Ezekiel and the passage in Revelation to see if this invasion by Gog and Magog can be the battle of Armageddon.

As the passage comparison shows below, there are just too many differences for them to be the same. The invasion of Gog and Magog cannot be the gathering of the forces of the Antichrist at Armageddon.

---

[94]. Spence and Exell, 285.

Ezekiel	Revelation
38:4 "And I will turn thee back…"	16:16 "And he gathered them together…"
38:8 "…against the mountains of Israel…"	16:16 "…into a place called in the Hebrew tongue Armageddon"
38:15 "And thou shalt come…out of the north parts…"	16:14 "…and of the whole world…"
39:2 "I will turn thee back and leave but the sixth part…"	19:21 "And the remnant were slain with the sword…"

The above comparison shows but a few of the contrasts between these two passages and helps show that the invasion of Gog and Magog cannot be the battle of Armageddon.

In Conclusion

Since the invasion of Gog and Magog cannot have already happened in past history and since it has to be in the end times, and since it has to happen before the battle of Armageddon, it seems that this event belongs either early in the Tribulation or no later than the half way point.

Chapter 15
Israel Believes

It's not that there is disagreement over whether Israel will one day be saved as the Apostle Paul makes it very clear that they will when he wrote "All Israel will be saved" (Romans 11:26). But there is disagreement over who "Israel" actually is in the mind of Paul, the New Testament writer. And when this will actually happen.

Is "Israel" the country of Israel in the days of the Bible or is it referring to modern day Jews that are alive in the end times? Is the reference to anyone of Jewish bloodline or is it a reference to those that are saved? And of course, there are some that wrongly believe that the church has replaced Israel but as we have already talked about and about to show, that is not taking the Scriptures literally or even seriously.

Well, when some of the leaders of the Jews evidently gave the impression that they knew they were saved because they were the descendants of Abraham, John the Baptist said "Bring forth therefore fruits worthy of repentance and begin not to say within yourselves, We have Abraham to our father (or we are Jews) for I say unto you That God is able of these stones to raise up children unto Abraham" (Luke 3:8). Even the Lord Jesus mentions this as when His own family came and was asking to see Him, He said that His family was actually those that believed "For whosoever shall do the will of God, the same is my brother and my sister and mother" (Mark 3:35).

These passages are making the point that just because someone is of the Jewish bloodline, does not mean that they are automatically saved and are not trying to make the point that the church is replacing Israel. Those who take a literal interpretation approach to the promises and prophecies to the Old Testament, which has already been shown to be correct, believe that the physical descendants of Abraham, Isaac, and Jacob will one day be restored not only in a right relationship with God but shall be the examples for all in how to serve the Lord.

The view that the church will replace Israel is usually referred to as *Replacement Theology* and is one of the basic underlying foundations of *Covenant Theology*. For example, the

Westminster Confession of Faith refers to the church as those of all ages which have been saved, from their point of view it was Israel in the Old Testament who have been replaced by the Church in the New Testament.[95]

    The church cannot be Israel for a variety of reasons and Dwight Pentecost list several in his book *Things to Come*.[96] He points out that Israel and Gentiles are actually contrasted in the New Testament rather than combined. This is very clear in the epistles of Paul "Brethren my heart's desire and prayer to God for Israel is, that they might be saved" (Romans 10:1). He also states that God is not done with Israel as Paul writes "I say then, Hath God cast away his people? God forbid. For I also am an Israelite, of the seed of Abraham…" (Romans 11:1). And of course, a study of the Abrahamic and Palestinian Covenants shows that for these to come true, the Lord will have to restore natural Israel and the actual seed of Abraham to the land.[97]

    Those who hold to replacement theology say that Christ has completely replaced Israel and that Israel will no longer inherit God's promises but that the church will sort of inherit them spiritually. Of course this is an example of non-literal interpretation gone wrong, where a theological system then forces the Scriptures into a wrong interpretation in order to fit its preconceived perspective.

    That God would swear His eternal love for Israel and then to cast them away forever and ignore all the details of His promises that He made to Abraham and Jacob and Moses and David is just not consistent with the God of the Bible.

    In taking the literal approach, it makes not only all the promises to Israel still able to be fulfilled in the future but helps students understand the passages that speak of Israel in the New Testament. For instance, the passage in Romans where Christians and the church are 'grafted in' make much more sense with the view that the root stock is Israel and believers are but now part of God's family. If Israel was to be set aside forever,

---

[95]. *Westminster Confession of Faith* (Glasgow, Scotland: Free Presbyterian Publications, 1958), 25.1.

[96]. Pentecost, 88.

[97]. Ibid., 90-91.

why would believers need to be grafted in? Notice the similar thoughts in Isaiah and Jeremiah.

Isaiah 59	Jeremiah 31
vs 21 "…this is my covenant with them…"	vs 33 "…this shall be the covenant that I will make with the house of Israel…"
vs 21 "…my words which I have put in thy mouth…"	vs 33 "…I will put my law in their inward parts and write it in their hearts…"
vs 21 "…from henceforth and for ever"	vs 33 "…and will be their God and they shall be my people"

So When Will Israel Be Saved?

Though there may have been Jewish political movements that have brought Israelites to the land, such as the Independence movement of the 1940's and 1950's, and there were other efforts along this line in past history, even near the end of the Roman Empire era, but there has never been a spiritual awakening and a return to Israel by Jews since the return of Jews in the days of Ezra and Nehemiah.

And so it seems that will remain the case, that is until God intervenes and begins to call His people home, both geographically and spiritually. And the passages that deal with this are numerous but perhaps the most prominent to the Christian today is the parable of the Fig Tree in Matthew 24.[98]

Regarding as to what the fig tree refers to and that it frankly must be Israel, here Chafer is quoted: "It is doubtless true that the fig tree represents in other Scriptures the nation of Israel, but there is no occasion for this meaning to be sought in the present use of that symbol. When the things of which Christ had just spoken, including even the beginnings of travail, begin to

---

[98]. Pentecost, 282.

come to pass, it may be accepted as certain that He is nigh, even at the doors".[99]

Now there has been disagreement over the word "*generation*" in the passage "Verily I say unto you, This generation shall not pass till all these things be fulfilled" (Matthew 24:34). As earlier discussed, many well meaning Christians thought that a 'generation' was forty years and when Israel became a nation in 1948, they just knew that the Lord would come before 1988. And when that didn't happen, they plugged in seventy years but at the writing of this book, the Lord hasn't returned. But as time as went on, especially in the last few decades, most have come to see that this refers to those that are alive during the tribulation, for that is the setting in which the parable is told.

It seems that sometime in the Tribulation, that God begins to work in the hearts of the Jews around the world and not only begin to draw them home but to work in their hearts spiritually. This is spoken of in Zechariah 8 - 14 and in Revelation 7 - 19.

An example verse would be "*I will pour out on the house of David and the inhabitants of Jerusalem a spirit of grace and supplication. They will look on me, the one they have pierced, and they will mourn for him as one mourns for an only child, and grieve bitterly for him as one grieves for a firstborn son*" (Zechariah 12:10).

The prophet Daniel also places this gathering of Israel during the Tribulation in his prophecy of weeks.[100] The "weeks" intend a meaning of seven years for a total of 490 years from when the Persian king gave the order to rebuild Jerusalem "*Seventy weeks are determined upon thy people and upon the holy city…*" (Daniel 9:24). The next verse sets out that near the end, with seven years still to go, that the Messiah would come but would be sacrificed "*…And after threescore and two weeks shall Messiah be cut off, but not for Himself…*" (Daniel 9:26a) saying that Christ will come but will not set up the kingdom as He was "cut off" short of fulfilling all the prophecy at this time because "*…the people of the prince that come shall destroy the holy city

---

[99]. Lewis Sperry Chafer, *Systematic Theology* (Grand Rapids: Kregel, 1976), 5:126-127.

[100]. Stanton, 184.

and the sanctuary and the end thereof shall be with a flood, and unto the end of the war of desolations are determined" (Daniel 9:26b). But after this interruption the Lord will return "even until the consummation and that determined shall be poured upon the desolate" (Daniel 9:27).

And it is during this time that the Lord will bring the faithful back to Jerusalem for "in truth and righteousness" (Zechariah 8:7), they will return. And even more specifically, the Bible says "I will put my Spirit in you and you will live, and I will settle you in your own land (Ezekiel 37:14). In fact, this next section will compare some thoughts from Matthew 24 and Ezekiel:

Ezekiel	Matthew
20:34 "And I will bring you out from a people and will gather you out of the countries wherein ye are scattered…"	24: 31 "And He shall send his angels with a great sound of a trumpet, and they shall gather together His elect…"
20:38 "And I will purge out from among you the rebels and them that transgress against me…"	25:32 "And before him shall be gathered all nations and He shall separate them one from another, as a shepherd divideth His sheep from the goats"
37:27 "My tabernacle also shall be with them yea, I will be their God and they shall be people"	25:34 "Then shall the King say unto them on His right hand, Come ye blessed of my Father, inherit the kingdom prepared for you from the foundation of the world"

And though this writer would agree that these verses are not speaking of the exactness of the timing concerning the gathering of Israel, they show the Lord's intent in the end times. I also think that there will be an increase of persecution for the Jews and that many return to Israel to escape persecution but the

Lord will use that to prepare their hearts spiritually. Dwight Pentecost says this part of prophecy is actually the whole point of the Lord's return.[101]

When During the Tribulation Will Israel Be Saved?

To begin to determine where to put this event in the end-times timeline, we will have to do some of what could be called bracketing. What is known to come before the event and where is that in the end-times timeline and what is known to come after the event and where is that in the end-times timeline?

What is known to come before Israel believing is that Israel makes a peace treaty with the Antichrist during the Tribulation. Obviously, if they were in belief, they would not be making a treaty with the Antichrist, so the question is where to place the first bracket. And it is the book of Daniel that sets this event "*And he shall confirm the covenant with many for one week: and in the midst of the week he shall cause the sacrifice and oblation to cease, and for the overspreading of abominations he shall make it desolate, even until the consummation, and that determined shall be poured upon the desolate*" (Daniel 9:27).

In explanation of this verse the Prophecy Study Bible says that there "is the signing of the seven-year covenant between "*the prince*" (of Daniel 9:25) and the city of Jerusalem and the Jews."[102] The explanation goes on to say that the Antichrist will break his covenant with Israel in the middle of the seven year tribulation and will stop the Jews worship practices and will go out of his way to defile the Temple. This is what most think Jesus was referring to when He spoke of the "*abomination of desolation*" (Matthew 24:15).[103]

So if the Antichrist breaks the covenant in "*midst of the week*" and the "*week*" represents seven years, then it can be said that Israel mostly remain in unbelief until around the three and a half year point of the Tribulation. But then at that point,

---

[101]. Pentecost, 281.

[102]. LaHaye, *Prophecy Study Bible*, 914.

[103]. Stanton, 318.

something happens. Why does the Antichrist turn on the Jews? Why does he stop the worship of God in the Jewish Temple? Why would he go out of his way to defile the Temple and desecrate it? Perhaps the answer is also found in Daniel in its references to a Seleucid king in the four hundred silent years between the Old and New Testaments.

Daniel 8 states that the *"rough goat is the king of Grecia"* and that his kingdom would be divided into four kingdoms, which history shows to have happened, with one kingdom being the Seleucid kingdom in Syria. The king of this kingdom was Antiochus Epiphanes who because of political unrest at his border with Egypt, blamed the Jews and began to persecute them, eventually taking Jerusalem itself and began turning the Jewish Temple into a Temple of Zeus.[104] And when he set up that statue of Zeus, with his face of course, this is what is referred to in Daniel 9:27 as the *"desolation"*.

So back to the question of why would the Antichrist turn on the Jews during the Tribulation? Perhaps for the same reason that Antiochus Epiphanes turned on the Jews in 279B.C., because they no longer were loyal to him and were looking to another.

If that is the case, who are the Jews looking to for deliverance? Who are they trusting in instead of the Antichrist? Who would make him so mad that he would go out of his way to permanently ruin a relationship with them and desecrate their Temple? I think the answer is the Lord Jesus!

Since it has already been established that the invasion by Gog and Magog happens during the Tribulation, it may be this attempted invasion that helps Israel see the Lord Jesus as the Messiah. In Ezekiel 38, after describing that the nations of the north come into the land of Israel to take spoil, that the Lord speaks out and steps in to stop and destroy them. Take a look at what happens in this passage and the next chapter.

---

[104]. Kevin Howard and Marvin Rosenthal, *The Feasts of the Lord: God's Prophetic Calendar from Calvary to the Kingdom* (Nashville: Thomas Nelson, 1997), 162.

Ezekiel 38

Verse 19	"For in my jealousy and in the fire of my wrath have I spoken, Surely in that day there shall be a great shaking in the land of Israel"
Verse 21	"And I will call for a sword against him throughout all my mountains, saith the Lord God; every man's sword shall be against his brother"
Verse 23	"Thus I will magnify myself, and sanctify myself and I will be known in the eyes of many nations, and they shall know that I am the Lord"

Ezekiel 39

Verse 7	"So will I make my holy name known in the midst of my people Israel; and I will not let them pollute my holy name any more and the heathen shall know that I am the Lord, the Holy One in Israel"
Verse 27	"When I have brought them again from the people and gathered them out of their enemies' lands, and am sanctified in them in the sight of many nations;"
Verse 29	"Neither will I hide my face any more from them: for I have poured out my spirit upon the house of Israel, saith the Lord God"

Though the beginning of these prophetic chapters deal with the invasion of Gog and Magog, the passage ends with a very clear point that Israel will realize that the Antichrist is not the Messiah as He destroys the armies of Gog and Magog and that causes them to believe on Christ. And this may be the event that opens their eyes to Christ.

In conclusion and to sort of lay out how all this might happen, let's look at a possible timeline. The last days will likely find an increase of anti-jewish sentiment or just flat out fear of the Jews in some countries, such as in some nations of Europe where the increasing population of Muslims has caused a disruption of their societies, where Jews had lived safely for decades but now are fearful.

And at the Rapture, with the removal of true Christians, who tend to look kindly on God's chosen people, the world may almost overnight, develop an animosity towards the Jews, also forcing many of them to escape to Israel.

Israel will evidently seem to be a safe destination, as the political leaders of Israel will have just signed a peace treaty with a major world leader, the Antichrist, but of course they don't know that yet. And in Israel itself, there is a resurgence of religious life, as the Jewish Temple is either rebuilt or is in the process of being built, a draw for every Jew. And since we know that Gog and Magog later invade to "take spoil", Israel is evidently doing well economically, some think getting rich for striking oil or finding gold deposits.

At first, the relationship with the Antichrist seems just a politically good move with both economic and religious benefits but as the Antichrist becomes jealous of God, who the Jews are worshipping, he begins to turn against them, if he wasn't from the beginning, which is likely so.

Somewhere during the middle years of the Tribulation, the countries identified as Gog and Magog determine that they need to invade Israel. As stated in the chapter on Gog and Magog, they come for "spoil" and perhaps also to reassert their political importance, and almost to put the Antichrist in his place. But instead of the Antichrist protecting Israel with military means as the treaty likely stated was his responsibility, Jesus Himself defends them and uses supernatural means to do so.

Could it be then that they see Jesus as the One whom they pierced and realize that Jesus was their Messiah after all? Could the Antichrist then for jealously, set up an image in the Jewish Temple to be worshipped which immediately shows the Jews that they have been led astray by a false prophet?

And remember that there just happens to be 144,000 Jewish preachers that have been preaching all throughout Israel and around the world to the Jews and anyone who would listen that Jesus was indeed the Messiah and that He's coming back again.

And though Daniel was told to "shut up" his book of prophecy until the end days, do these events put in the hearts of Jews to get out their scrolls and to discover the ancient book of Daniel and find themselves right in the middle of the story? And will they then realize that they have literally made a deal with the devil and then as many of the prophets said, and then look to the One who has loved them all along, that being Christ.

Will Christ appear to the Jews during the Tribulation to bring them to belief? I think so!

Chapter 16
The Abomination of Desolation

The "*Abomination of desolation*" is part of the end-time timeline in Matthew 24 as Jesus walks His disciples through what will happen in the last days. And this seems to very clearly be a continuation of the prophecy originally given to Daniel. It is referring to perhaps as many as three events, all defiling the Temple, with the first being done by Antiochus Epiphanes before the time of Christ in the era between the close of the Old Testament and the beginning of the New Testament, as described in the previous chapter. It may also refer to the Romans destroying Jerusalem and the Temple in 70A.D., which seems to be a swift chastisement of Jerusalem for rejecting Christ. And lastly it refers to the actions taken by the Antichrist during the time of the Tribulation.

The Hebrew word for "abomination" is *shaqats*, which means '*to be filthy*' or '*to abhor*' and the term is from the Septuagint.[105] Abomination in the Old Testament is generally thought of as idolatry. This would match Antiochus' actions as he set up a statue of Zeus, and might refer to the Romans setting up their standard or symbolic flag over the Temple after they destroyed it and certainly likely refers to the Antichrist setting up a statue of either himself or the devil, as John speaks of "*And deceiveth them that dwell on the earth by the means of those miracles which he had power to do in the sight of the beast; saying to them that dwell on the earth that they should make an image to the beast…*" (Revelation 13:14).

The use of the word "Abomination" carries with it a clear and purposeful effort to convey a hateful act meant to offend and challenge whatever was the normal view of what was sacred or holy. For this is exactly what Antiochus the Seleucid king intended by offering a pig on the altar and sprinkling its blood in the Holy of Holies. Swine were seen as unclean and a pig was literally seen as the most unclean animal there was to the Jew, picturing all that was dirty and filthy. It was pure contempt.

---

[105]. Spence and Exell, 434.

Here is another case of near and far prophecy, as discussed in earlier chapters and it seems there are many lessons to learn about the one day future fulfillment of this horrendous act by the Antichrist if one looks at the previous act done by Antiochus Epiphanes in the inter-testamental period (inter-testamental refers to the four hundred year era between the book of Malachi and the book of Matthew).

The First Fulfillment of the Abomination of Desolation

This section will begin with Daniel 11, although Daniel 9:27 also refers to it. Daniel 11 tells again of a kingdom that is divided into four parts "his kingdom shall be broken and shall be divided toward the four winds (meaning a north, south, east, west). It tells us that the "*king of the south shall be strong*" (Daniel 11:5), which is a reference to the Ptolemy kingdom in Egypt.[106] And it tells of the "*king of the north*" (Daniel 11:13), which is a reference to the Greek-Syrian kingdom called the Seleucid kingdom under King Antiochus Epiphanes. And a detailed study of this passage would show that the war between the Seleucid kingdom in Syria and the Ptolemy kingdom in Egypt was a perfect fulfillment of the passage, including the king of the north desecrating the Temple.

Antiochus Epiphanes, who ruled from Syria, outlawed all forms of Jewish worship, including circumcision, sacrifices, keeping the Sabbath and more. And he set up statues and idols of different Greek gods in the Jewish Temple and offered animals to them that would offend the Jews. The offering of a swine on the Jewish altar was loathsome and abhorrent to the Jewish people. And Daniel writes about this again "*And arms shall stand on his part and they shall pollute the sanctuary of strength and shall take away the daily sacrifice and they shall place the abomination that maketh desolate*" (Daniel 11:31).

Whether this was the placement of idols to false gods or the offering of the pig and smearing it's blood in the Holy Place or just a combination of all these things is less clear but the act of disrespect with malice certainly got the intended effect. If that

---

[106]. LaHaye, *Prophecy Study Bible*, 916.

was to picture how the Antichrist will act, no wonder the Jews abandon him.

The Second Fulfillment of the Abomination of Desolation

This section will move back now to Daniel 9 where it seems the reference to the second fulfillment is mentioned, woven in with details about the first. That the first fulfillment is part of the prophecy is clear from *"Grecia"* being mentioned leading up to this in chapter 8. And then chapter 9 states that *"the people of the prince that shall come shall destroy the city and the sanctuary and the end thereof shall be…"* (Daniel 9:26).

One proof that this is the Romans in 70A.D. is of course, what was just mentioned, that being that they destroyed the city. They are the only ones who have destroyed the city since the Babylonians, and of course, Daniel was written after that event.

And later in Daniel 9:27, the pronoun *"he"* which is the one who causes the sacrifices to cease *"for the overspreading of abominations"* must refer back to the preceding verse and must be the *"prince"* of the armies that destroyed Jerusalem.[107]

Another proof would be the Lord Jesus Himself referring to what seems to be a near judgment *"And when ye shall see Jerusalem compassed with armies then know that the desolation thereof is nigh"* (Luke 21:20).

And so if Daniel was primarily speaking of what would happen soon in his day, that being the desolation of the Seleucid king, then it would also make sense that Jesus would be speaking primarily of the desolation of the Romans, just forty years from when the Jews rejected Him as their king. The passage in Luke goes on speaking of things that cannot be in the Tribulation but involved things that set up the *"time of the Gentiles"* (Luke 21:24). That this was the Roman General Titus in 70A.D. seems clear.[108]

Remember that we looked in the introduction chapters that prophecy wasn't intended to be easy but to offer deep things for those interested in the challenge, showing all the time just

---

[107]. Pentecost, 172.

[108]. Pentecost., 276.

how much God is in control of all things, including the nations of the earth.

The Third Fulfillment of the Abomination of Desolation

And now that it is evident that the first two fulfillments were really just foreshadows of what will happen during the Tribulation, we can with more understanding, look to the days of the Antichrist. To start with, Jesus spoke of the "abomination of desolation" and said *"When ye therefore shall see the Abomination of desolation spoken of by Daniel the prophet stand in the holy place"* (Matthew 24:15). Here the Lord Jesus places this event in the future "when ye therefore shall see" and refers to the one who is desolating "standing in the holy place".

This has to be the Antichrist, as it is the future and Antiochus is long dead and it cannot be referring to the Romans as there is no record of the Roman General Titus standing in the holy place for the Temple. In fact, the Temple was burned down before he ever entered the city, either set on fire by Roman siege engines or set on fire by the priests themselves to keep in being violated by the Romans. So there has to be another event in mind that the Roman destruction of the Temple in 70A.D. And there hasn't been a Jewish Temple since then.

Further proof that this was not referring to the Romans is that Daniel was told that some of these prophecies would not happen until the end-times *"But thou Daniel, shut up the words and seal the book, even to the time of the end…"* (Daniel 12:4). And to call 70A.D. the end times is just ridiculous. Daniel was told to seal the book again in verse 9 but that people would understand more about the Lord's second coming after His first coming.[109]

And so since we are left with no other choice than the prophecy of Jesus in Matthew 24 being the future Antichrist, let's see what we can learn? As we have studied, the "week" mentioned in Daniel represents the Antichrist's seven-year reign. That reign will include signing a peace treaty with Israel and some other nations, including, it seems, his own, and evidently

---

[109]. LaHaye, *Prophecy Study Bible*, 921.

guaranteeing safety for Israel. And it would seem that also included allowing the Jews to rebuild the Temple.

And three and a half years into it the Antichrist stops the sacrifice in the Temple. By the way, if the "sacrifice and offering" are ended, then they first have to have started. And if it's going to start, then the Jews have to have the temple. So this indicates that the construction and use of the temple is one of the issues covered in the seven-year Covenant.

It seems that this ban on worship will not just be for Jewish temple as the Antichrist will forbid and abolish all religious worship as we're told in Revelation that he actually turns on the very world religion that at first endorsed him. But all pretense is removed as the Antichrist declares himself God and requires worship of himself, with suppression, persecution, and even death to all who won't bow to him.

We're also told in Revelation that the Antichrist will set up an idol that people need to bow to and this is the worst of the "*Abomination of Desolation*" (Daniel 11:31). Jesus said that we'd better understand, because He was placing this event in the future and that this would be a terrible time and that Jews should flee Jerusalem. In the Roman siege, it was impossible to flee as the city was surrounded but in the days of the Antichrist, it will evidently be possible to flee and the Jews seem to flee to the ancient rock fortress of Petra in southern Jordan.

As far as knowing whether the Antichrist will set up a statue, Jesus said they would see it "*standing in the holy place.*" Daniel 11:31 says the Antichrist "*places there the Abomination of Desolation.*" Daniel 12:11 says that "*the Abomination of Desolation is set up.*" He places it, he sets it up and it stands there, so it's some kind of standing object. And Revelation 13 says it's an image and then even more scary, is that it is either possessed or something, for we're told that it talks. "*And he deceives those who dwell on the earth by those signs which he was granted to do in the sight of the Beast, telling those who dwell on the earth to make an image to the Beast who was wounded by the sword and lived. He was granted power to give breath to the Image of the Beast, that the Image of the Beast should both speak and cause as many as would not worship the Image of the Beast to be killed*" (Revelation 13:14–15).

Whether it is a possessed image of himself, a hologram of his father the devil, or something that we can't even imagine, this image is intended to take the place of God's presence in the Holy Place in the Temple and to be worshipped as God.

Illustration of the Antichrist and False Prophet with an idol of himself in the Jewish Temple. This is one of the possible interpretations of the Abomination of Desolation that will occur mid way through the Tribulation.

Chapter 17
The Two Witnesses

Revelation 11 begins with the Lord talking about the Temple in Jerusalem. It is by now under the control of the Antichrist. So it must be that God is fully aware that there will need to be a new Temple and is having John symbolically taking measurements for it. This thought is validated by the next verse *"But the court which is without the temple leave out, and measure it not for it is given unto the Gentiles and the holy city shall they tread under foot forty and two months"* (Revelation 11:2). The verse also mentions that this is three and a half years, the second half of the Tribulation which started with the Antichrist breaking his treaty with Israel and then taking the Jewish Temple as his own.[110]

And so in the middle of the Tribulation when it seems that all is at its worst, Scripture shows that there are *"two witnesses"* that come forth and preach the Gospel right there in Jerusalem in the Temple in spite of the Antichrist. So what can be known about them? I love that God always sends a prophet or preacher to remind people that He still has a message and that people still have a choice. The appearance of these two witnesses is not only interesting but inspiring!

The Length of Their Ministry

Scripture states that they preach for *"a thousand two hundred and threescore days"* (Revelation 11:3), which is three and a half years. Now I might suggest that perhaps they have been preaching before the mid-way point of the Tribulation but have been directed to Jerusalem itself at least by then.[111] Perhaps they were sent down from heaven or also called to preach by God when the 144,000 Jewish witnesses began, perhaps even being their teachers before they set out to take the Gospel around the world.

---

[110]. Phillips, *Exploring Revelation*, 1380.

[111]. Ibid., 146.

The Spiritual Power of Their Ministry

They are compared to the "*two olive trees and the two candlesticks standing before the God of the earth*" (Revelation 11:4) which is a reference to the parable-like visions in the book of Zechariah. John Phillips says this speaks of their supernatural power and the backing of God Himself in their sustainment just like God took care of Noah, Abraham, Elisha and all who He calls to preach for Him.[112]

Vs 5 shows just how powerful they are "*And if any man will hurt them, fire proceedeth out of their mouth and devoureth their enemies and if any man will hurt them, he must in this manner be killed*" (Revelation 11:5). So their preaching is so powerful that it literally consumes the wicked.[113] Can you just imagine how frustrated and angry they make the Antichrist?

The Purpose of Their Ministry

It seems that verses 6-7 of Revelation 11 show that the purpose is to make it clear to the world that judgment is coming. Verse 6 states "*These have power to shut heaven that it rain not in the days of their prophecy and have powers over waters to turn them to blood, and to smite the earth with all plagues, as often as they will*". And verse 7 begins "*And when they have finished their testimony…*", showing that the above mentioned miraculous judgments was to give testimony of God and His power. It can remind readers of how Elijah called down fire from heaven to show the people of Israel that God was more powerful than Baal and it can remind readers of how Moses brought plagues upon Egypt to show them that the Hebrew God was more powerful than the Egyptian ones. These two witnesses are a turning point in Israel's belief and to some degree, perhaps Gentiles around the world, that look on in wonder that they withstand the Antichrist and cannot be killed and silenced.

---

[112]. Pentecost, 147.

[113]. Albert Garner, *Revelation*, Baptist Commentary (Lakeland, FL: Blessed Hope Foundation, 1985), 186.

The Persecution They Receive for Their Ministry

Those in the employment of the Antichrist will try to kill them, as it stated in verse 5, but now in verse 7 they are confronted and finally killed *"And when they shall have finished their testimony, the beast that ascendeth out of the bottomless pit shall make war against them and shall overcome them and kill them"* (Revelation 11:7).

And in the next verse, they were given no honor even in death *"And their dead bodies shall lie in the street of the great city…where also our Lord was crucified"* (Revelation 11:8). And verse 9 shows that upon their death, the entire world celebrates. No one generally likes being confronted by their sin and all those that have already sided with the Antichrist will hate these two prophets of God.

The Panic That Occurs When They Rise from the dead

Their bodies lay in the dust for three days, more likely from fear of approaching them more than anything else but Scripture says that after these three days, they will be resurrected and rise to heaven. Can you just imagine the news footage, showing them standing up and being taken to heaven after the Antichrist had claimed victory over them?

So Who Could the Two Witnesses Be?

This is one of those topics in prophecy where there are many different ideas.[114] There is the symbolic approach where the two witnesses only represent the church which some think have not yet been raptured out of the world and still remain, and upon the symbolic slaying of the witnesses, the church is finally taken home to heaven.

But this cannot be the interpretation, for one, we have already established that the prophecies concerning Israel are literal and intended to be taken just as they seem, as a real event somewhere in the future.

---

[114]. Pentecost, 304.

Secondly, also previously pointed out, the language used is just too specific. There are two witnesses, not an unknown figure, they will preach for a specific number of days, not a generic time frame, and the details of what happens after their death would not be necessary if they but represented some people group. Yes, sometimes the Bible does uses symbolism but when details are given it is not to be taken symbolically but literally.

Thirdly, the witnesses both perish at one time. Dwight Pentecost makes a good point, saying "The witnesses all perish at one point of time so that their testimony ceases. And yet it is shown that the believing remnant, although decimated by the activities of the Beast, will continue throughout the period unto the coming of the Lord. The continuing witness seems to argue against identifying them with the remnant".[115] By this Pentecost is showing how they cannot be symbolic for there will be a remnant of believers that survive unto the end on the earth and the fact that the witnesses are slain and then resurrected and taken to heaven, only show that they are literal men.

The remaining view then is that they are two real people. But who are they? Of course, they could be two men that are not brought back from the days of Scripture as there is nothing to prevent that from being the case. But it is the overwhelming passages on Elijah that make people think that these two witnesses are the ultimate fulfillment of Elijah come to prepare the way of the Lord.

The Old Testament does predict that Elijah will come again "*Behold I will send you Elijah the prophet before the coming of the great and dreadful day of the Lord*" (Malachi 4:5). Now of course, some thought that John the Baptist was Elijah come again but John clearly denied being the fulfillment of that prophecy "*And they asked him, What then? Art thou Elijah? And saith I am not. Art thou that prophet? And he answered No*" (John 1:21).

Tim LaHaye perhaps gives the best discussion of this in the Prophecy Study Bible.[116] He says that Elijah seems to be an overwhelming choice and then regarding the other witness, that

---

[115]. Pentecost, 305.

[116]. LaHaye, *Prophecy Study Bible*, 1381.

Enoch and Moses are considered. The reservation about Enoch is that the Bible says he was translated so that he would not see death, that leaving Moses, which seems to fit a lot of connections in other passages of the Bible.

For instance, it was Elijah and Moses at the Mount of Transfiguration "*And behold, there appeared unto them Moses and Elijah talking with Him*" (Matthew 17:3). And Moses and Elijah would of course, represent the law and the prophets, a phrase used often by the Lord "*On these two commandments hang all the law and the prophets*" (Matthew 22:40).

And lastly, since devouring fire is mentioned and plagues, those two items fit the ministry of Elijah and Moses, fire being from Elijah's ministry and plagues being from Moses' ministry.[117] Regardless of who they are, they are a spiritual shot in the arm to the those who come to Christ during the Tribulation and the beginning of doomsday for those who hate God.

Two witnesses will preach in Jerusalem during the Tribulation,

---

[117]. Ibid., 1381.

Chapter 18
The Campaign of Armageddon

To anyone who reads a Bible, attends a Bible teaching church, or for that matter pays attention to even Hollywood, nothing says the end like the word Armageddon. It is found specifically in Revelation "And he gathered them together into a place called in the Hebrew tongue Armageddon" (Revelation 16:16). This is looked at by most of Christianity and for that matter, the whole world as the last battle on earth between good and evil, with God and good having victory.

Armageddon is the ancient Greek word *Harmagedon* which became later in Latin *Armagedon*. It is originally from the Hebrew *Har Megiddo*, a real valley in northern Israel. The valley runs mostly north-south along a stretch of road called *Via Maris* which means the 'Way of the Sea' and was a major international highway in the ancient world.

On any Bible map, one can see the road ran from Egypt in the south to Damascus in Syria and then on to Babylon to the east. It was used as a primary trade route, affecting the economy of everyone linked to it and, of course, was a route taken by armies of the day, who were restricted to roads with fresh water along the route. And Megiddo had amble water supply, including underground tunnels that moved water not only into the city but into pools as well, in order to water the horses of travelers.[118]

And in the middle of this route lay the twelve mile long valley of Israel and in the middle of that lay the city of Megiddo, which not only overlooked the valley but was a choke point, meaning that whoever controlled Megiddo, controlled the highway and thus everyone and everything that wanted to use it.

And so as one can imagine, many battles took place in this valley. In 1479B.C., the Egyptian Pharaoh Thutmose III came there to assert dominion over territories in Canaan and paused near Megiddo as they referred to it as *"the flat valley of Jezreel"*.[119] The area is also mentioned often in the Scriptures and often as a battlefield. For instance, Joshua mentions it as the

---

[118]. J. A. Thompson, *The Bible and Archaeology* (Grand Rapids: Eerdmans, 1962), 109.

[119]. Leonard Cottrell, *The Lost Pharoahs* (New York: Columbia University Press, 2005), 46.

Israelites took the land *"And Manasseh had in Issachar and in Asher…and the inhabitants of Megiddo and her towns, even three countries"* (Joshua 17:11). So evidently Joshua fought in this area. And 1 Kings shows how Solomon saw Megiddo's military potential and built it up as a garrison. And later 2 Kings shows an example of a battle near there *"In his days Pharaoh-Necho king of Egypt went up against the king of Assyria to the river Eurphrates and King Josiah went against him; and he slew him at Megiddo…"* (2 Kings 23:29). In fact, even Napoleon Bonaparte, the emperor of France, upon visiting the site, called it the perfect battlefield. [120]

And so with its military history in ages gone by, it is no surprise that it just happens to be where the Antichrist will gather his forces to take on God and Jerusalem. The prophet Zechariah records God saying *"Behold the day of the Lord cometh…For I will gather all nations against Jerusalem to battle…"* (Zechariah 14:1-2). The prophet Joel then names the location *"I will also gather all nations and will bring them down into the valley of Jehoshaphat…"* (Joel 3:2), which is another name for the valley.

Who Will Fight In the Campaign of Armageddon?

As to who participates in this battle, it is a list of almost every alliance or direction on earth and they are all gathering against God. The forces of the Antichrist will be there as it is clear that he is leading them *"And I saw the beast, and the kings of the earth, and their armies, gathered together to make war against him that sat on the horse…"* (Revelation 19:19).

These *"kings"*, if not the kings of the entire earth, are at least the *"kings"* or leaders of those nations from which the Antichrist came out of, the ten nation confederacy from which he emerged politically. This view seems to line up perfectly with Daniel's prophecy.[121] And by this time, it seems that his influence has grown beyond the revived old Roman or old Ottoman empire, for it seems that his influence, if not his rule,

---

[120]. Stephen M. Miller, *Stephen M. Miller's Illustrated Bible Dictionary* (Ulrichsville, OH: Barbour, 2013), 23.

[121]. LaHaye, *Prophecy Study Bible*, 1393.

has spread beyond his initial borders. This next section will compare the kings in Revelation to the prophecy of Daniel.

Daniel 7	Revelation 17
vs 20 "And of the ten horns that were in his head…"	vs 12 "And <u>the ten horns</u> which thou sawest are ten kings…"
vs 20 "And of the ten horns that were in his head, and of the other which came up and before whom three fell…"	vs 10 "And there are seven kings, five are <u>fallen,</u> and one is, and the other is not yet come…"
vs 21 "…and the same horn made war with the saints…"	vs 14 "These shall <u>make war with the Lamb</u>…"

    There may also be remnants of the northern confederacy, namely Russia or Gog and Magog and its allies that had tried to take Israel but were turned back and it would seem quite natural for them to try again, allied with what seems to be a world-wide coalition. And there also comes the armies from the east *"And the sixth angel poured out his vial upon the great river Euphrates and the water thereof was dried up, that the way of the kings of the east might be prepared"* (Revelation 16:12).

    As to who *"the kings of the east"* are, some insight is given by the statement that the river Euphrates must be dried up for them to proceed. The Euphrates has often been understood the world over to separate the east from the west.[122] So the *"kings of the east"* must be at least east of the Euphrates. Now it is possible that they are no further east than modern day Iran as *"kings from the east"* did likely refer to those from the Persian empire in the days of Christ birth but those nations seem to have already been mentioned as those in league with Gog and Magog *"Persia, Ethiopia, and Libya with them…"* (Ezekiel 38:5). But these nations may have already been defeated with Gog and

---

[122]. Pentecost, 1391.

Magog. And though remnants might remain, they cannot be a major threat. So who might the Scriptures be referring to?

Armageddon War

So are the kings of the east the nations that readers today might think of as from the far east? The use of the phrase "north parts" which can be translated "*far north*" gives license to ask if the "*kings of the east*" are from the 'far east'. Some might initially say that the lands of China and Japan and the Far East are not on the Biblical radar but that would be incorrect. For instance China is mentioned in the end times when Israel is restored and if those far east lands are mentioned in the millennial time period, then it should not come as a surprise to find them mentioned in the Tribulational time period "*Behold, these shall come from far and lo, these from the north and from the west and these from the land of Sinim (far east)*" (Isaiah 49:12).

That the "*kings*" mentioned and the lands they come from must be from the 'Far East' is seen upon a close look at Revelation 16:12. The phrase "that the way of the kings of the east might be prepared" could be translated as 'In order that the roadway of the royal rulers from the land of the rising sun might be made ready'.[123]

---

[123]. Garner, *Revelation*, 267.

When Will The Campaign of Armageddon Take Place?

As to the timing of the battle of Armageddon, again some parameters seem to put it into place. First, the passages involved cannot refer to some past event in Israel's history as there is nothing even close that has already happened. There just have not been any invasions, where large alliances from the north, south, east and west arrive to fight a common foe. Yes, there have been invasions of Israel, perhaps more than any country in history, but none that match the prophecies in Daniel and Ezekiel and thus Revelation.[124]

If Ezekiel 37-39 starts with the invasion of Gog and Magog, which happens sometime during the Tribulation, and then slowly transitions into the Battle of Armageddon, then not only does the context put us at the end of the Tribulation, but right before they are restored into the land. This would then place the event at the end of the Tribulation. When it is placed there, all of a sudden, the whole timeline of Revelation then falls into place, with the battle is described in Revelation chapters 16-19.

There is some confusion, and this writer admits that it can be, that at the end of the Millennium, Gog and Magog is mentioned again *"And shall go out to deceive the nations which are in the four quarters of the earth, Gog and Magog..."* (Revelation 20:8).

My suggestion is that this must be a reference to the old world and its attitude toward the Lord. And John the Apostle used it as a reference to the age old enemies of Israel, perhaps more with the similarity in mind of their defeat than who they were. For just as the Lord quickly and easily destroyed Gog and Magog during the Tribulation, the Lord is said to bring fire to destroy them *"...and fire came down from God out of heaven, and devoured them"* (Revelation 20:9). And we take into consideration that the farther John looks out into the future, there seems to less details in his observations. The start of the Tribulation seems to be covered by a play by play description but

---

[124]. Pentecost, 345.

that begins to wind down near the end of the Tribulation and maybe God Himself speeds up time as Matthew 24:22 says *"And except those days should be shortened, there should no flesh be saved: but for the elect's sake those days shall be shortened"*.

And the mention of Gog and Magog must be a different event as that described earlier as it has different details. Mostly that after the battle of Armageddon, Christ begins His judgment on earth and sets up His kingdom and after the battle mentioned in Revelation 20, the Great White Throne Judgment takes place and believers are then in the Millennium.[125] These cannot be the same two events.[126]

And here is an event where no details are given about Gog and Magog or the battle itself and as we have discussed, this lack of details does allow some symbolism or for its mention to be generic in reference.

So with the invasion of Gog and Magog near the middle of the Tribulation and having set the battle in Revelation 20 at the end of the Millennium, it seems that the battle of Armageddon takes place at the end of the Tribulation and literally ushers in the return of Christ.

What Happens In The Campaign of Armageddon?

As to what happens, a vivid account is given in Revelation 19. In verse 11, the Lord appears in the heavens *"And I saw heaven opened and behold a white horse and he that sat upon him was called Faithful and True, and in righteousness He doth judge and make war"*. Next, the passage gives a description of the Lord in verse 12-13 and then given the report of who is coming with Him in verse 14 *"And the armies which were in heaven followed Him upon white horses clothed in fine linen, white and clean"*. And the battle is joined in verse 15 *"And out of His mouth goeth a sharp sword, that with it He should smite the nations and He shall rule them with a rod of iron and He treadeth the wine press of the fierceness and wrath of Almighty God"*.

---

[125]. LaHaye, *Prophecy Study Bible*, 1400.

[126]. Pentecost, 349.

Verse 17 tells of an angel calling scavengers *"And I saw an angel standing in the sun and he cried with a loud voice saying to all the fowls that fly in the midst of heaven, Come and gather yourselves together unto the supper of the great God"*. And the angel continues in verse 18 *"That ye may eat the flesh of kings and the flesh of captains and the flesh of mighty men and the flesh of horses and them that sit on them and the flesh of all men, both free and bond, both small and great"*.

Verse 19 states that *"the beast"* was still defiant *"And I saw the beast and the kings of the earth and their armies, gathered together to make war against him that sat on the horse and against his army"*. And then verse 20 tells of the outcome of *"the Beast"* or the Antichrist *"And the beast was taken and with him the false prophet that wrought miracles before him, with which he deceived them that had received the mark of the beast and them that worshipped his image. These both were cast both alive into a lake of fire burning with brimstone"*.

And verse 21 goes on *"And the remnant were slain with the sword of Him that sat upon the horse which sword proceeded out of His mouth…"*.

And after this passage, Revelation chapter 20 states that the devil is bound and cast into the *"bottomless pit"* for a thousand years, which, of course lines up with the literal view of the length of the Millennium.[127] This allows us to have bracketed the Battle of Armageddon again as it has to happen before the one thousand years of the Millennium but after all the other events of the Tribulation. For if satan is bound and the Antichrist and false prophet are removed, then the Tribulation is over. So it has to be the final event of the Tribulation and before the some of the judgments and certainly before the one thousand year Millennium starts.

So What Happens?

It seems that though the Antichrist arises to power from a small country in a confederation outside of Israel, he seems to be

---

[127]. Paul N. Benware, *Understanding End Times Prophecy: A Comprehensive Approach*, rev. ed. (Chicago: Moody, 2006), 125.

drawn to Israel. We already know that he was in Jerusalem when he took over the Temple and we know that most Jews have fled south to Petra in southern Jordan.

And remember that the Antichrist knows good and well who his enemy is as it seems that Jesus Himself had likely appeared to save Israel from the invasion from Gog and Magog. And though we can only speculate what all the sermon topics were that were preached on by the two witnesses that show up in Jerusalem, I think they openly expose the Antichrist for who he is. If they were anything like Elijah, who took on King Ahab or Moses, who took on Pharaoh or John the Baptist who took on King Herod, we can only imagine how the Antichrist is mentioned by name and exposed for his wickedness and that he the preachers promise that he will be dealt with when the Lord returns.

And perhaps because of that very preaching, or because God's wrath is at this point unbearable, or as the Scriptures say, that God Himself draws him there, the Antichrist begins to gather his forces to face down the coming Lord. And where could you gather a large army from around the world? Well, there is but just one place in Israel, that being the old Valley of Jezreel, known as the Valley of Meggido…Armageddon!

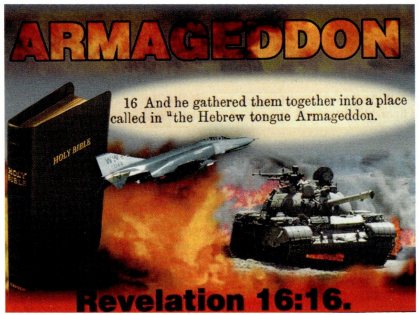

The battle of Armageddon is more of a last ditch effort campaign by the Antichrist to hold on to his power and then lastly to take a stand against Christ Himself. At the end of Armageddon, the Lord Jesus takes full control of the earth, rescuing the saints that have been saved during the Tribulation and judging the wicked.

Chapter 19
The Lord's Return

The return of Christ is often viewed as a simple concept with complicated details. And to some degree, I agree. That the Lord will return one day is understood throughout all or orthodox Christendom. But that doesn't mean there isn't some disagreement on the details. That is likely because of the confusion between the coming of the Lord to rapture or take the saints home to glory before the Tribulation and His full return when Christ comes to earth at the end of the Tribulation to defeat satan, the Antichrist and their allies and to set up His Millennial kingdom.

The Second Coming

Perhaps it would be helpful to look at the Second coming of Christ as a series of events, culminating with Jesus actually coming all the way to earth at Jerusalem at the end of the Tribulation. First, Jesus comes to the clouds to call the Christians home and then I think He makes His presence in heaven or the skies clear during the Tribulation, especially by the mid-way point and we find that from that point on, that those on the earth who have sided with the Antichrist openly challenge Him as John tells us "*And (they) blasphemed the God of Heaven…*" (Revelation 16:11. And then at the end of the seven years of Tribulation, which fulfills Daniel's seventy weeks, Christ comes to put an end to the Antichrist's reign and to rescue the saints, restore the Jews to the promised land and more.

So a Christian can look forward to the second coming and a believer in the Tribulation can look forward to the second coming for though they are separated by seven years, they are when Christ appears to begin to bring an end to all things.

The Kingdom of God

Another interesting discussion is that some get confused with the passages in the Gospels that speak about the kingdom of heaven or the kingdom of God having already come.

And it is usually brought up that the Bible says that Christ already rules in hearts. This has led some, mostly the Catholic church, to simply ignore the second coming of Christ, as they just don't see a need, as they would say that Christ already rules in the hearts of those that follow Him.

On this, let's first deal with the difference between a spiritual rule and a physical return. Yes, when Christ came the first time in the Gospels, He did to some extent, bring the Kingdom of Heaven to earth. And there was a sincere offer to the Jews to accept Him as their Messiah and if they would have accepted, Christ would have fulfilled all the promises made to them.[128] But they did not and instead crucified Him, postponing the coming Millennial kingdom to the end of the age. But truly, for a time while the Lord was here on earth, John the Baptist could rightly and truly say, *"Behold the Lamb"* and preach the kingdom.

And concerning the *"kingdom of God"* in our hearts, yes, the Lord does speak of that also *"And when He was demanded of the Pharisees about when the kingdom of God should come, He answered them and said, The kingdom of God cometh not with observation: Neither shall they say, Lo here! or, lo there! for, behold the kingdom of God is within you"* (Luke 17:20-21).

Here the Lord is responding to a group of people, the Pharisees, who were waiting for that physical kingdom with no thought of the need for a regenerated heart. And so to them, the Lord focuses on their spiritual need. But this was not the Lord saying there would be no physical kingdom one day.[129] This is no different than the Lord telling the rich young ruler that he needed to go and sell all that he had. It is not that everyone who wants to follow Christ must sell all that they have but just this rich young ruler, because the passage in Matthew 19 says that Jesus said this specifically to him because he evidently loved his many possessions.

---

[128]. McClain, 187.

[129]. Richard Pinelli, "The Kingdom of God: The Best News You Could Hear!," Life, Hope & Truth, https://lifehopeandtruth.com/prophecy/kingdom-of-god/ (accessed November 28, 2017).

So yes, the kingdom was partially present when Christ was here on earth and yes, the kingdom of God should reign in hearts, but that is not what the Bible is referring to when it speaks of the Lord's return to set up His kingdom. Jesus so much as said so *"In my Father's house are many mansions: if it were not so, I would have told you. I go to prepare and place for you. And if I go and prepare a place for you, I will come again and receive you unto myself that where I am, there ye may be also"* (John 14:2-3). He told His disciples that He would come again and that there would be a real kingdom and as theologian Alva McClain puts it "should not be confused with the spiritual kingdom" that is offered to anyone immediately upon belief.[130]

Details of the Second Coming

So now that it has been established that when Scripture speaks of the Lord's return, it is referring to a literally, physical return, we can now move on the details of that, including the two phrases of His return.

As stated, the first phase of the second coming is solely to rapture His saints and take them home to heaven where they shall be rewarded for their faithfulness and enjoy the marriage supper of the Lamb while the rebellious earth is judged and the unbelieving Jews are brought back into the fold. But even thinking of this wonderful event, and even though believers often refer to the Lord's coming to gather the saints, and truly, this will be the most important day in our lives, this is not really the end of the second coming. It is complete when the Lord returns to the earth one day in all the ways that believers imagine, physically, literally, majestically, royally to deal with all injustice and to establish a righteous kingdom and kingship on the earth.[131]

And for some details of this event, Matthew 24 gives a wider perspective than Revelation 19. Matthew 24 gives a sort of wide angle view, allowing readers to see many things going on as the Lord returns, almost a world view of the event, while

---

[130]. McClain, 374.

[131]. McClain, 477.

Revelation focuses on the coming of Christ with the purpose of defeating satan and the Antichrist.

A Timeline of Events from Matthew 24

In verses 5-7, as was already discussed, this is the early years of the Tribulation where the four horsemen of Revelation 6 are released on the earth, including the Antichrist, who rides this white horse. And verse 8 gives reassurance of that *"All these are the beginning of sorrows"*.

Verses 9-10 states that persecution will increase like the earth has never seen for anyone that names the name of God or Christ, which will bring persecution to the Jew, who the world knows is God's people, but also on any believing Gentiles who turn to Christ and refuse the mark of the beast. This division between those that follow Christ and the Antichrist become so prevalent that people will turn on their own families.

And verse 11 likely is a reference to the false prophet that arises during the Tribulation, who works for the Antichrist and satan, giving a pretense of religion but really preparing the people of the world to worship satan himself. The Pulpit Commentary states this very thing in pointing out that it has always been satan's plan to corrupt and deceive the very people God wishes to save by leading them astray with false prophets and proof of that is the Old Testament and New Testament are filled with examples of them and warnings about them.[132]

Verse 14 has to be referring to the evangelist ministry and preaching of the 144,000 that Revelation tells about as it says "And this Gospel of the kingdom shall be preached in all the world for a witness unto all nations and then shall the end come". This verse connects the Gospel going around the world and the end times calling of God's sealed servants from the twelve tribes to spread the Word. Also notice that they are preaching the *"Gospel of the Kingdom"* which was what was preached in the days of John the Baptist and Christ before the rejection. This is a clear reference that this is in the Tribulation, otherwise known as

---

[132]. Spence and Exell, 432.

the time of Jacob's trouble (Jeremiah 30:7) and Daniel's seventieth week (Daniel 9:24-27).

The "*Abomination of Desolation*" mentioned in verse 15 marks the mid-point of the seven year Tribulation for Daniel clearly states that the Antichrist will break his covenant with the Jews half way through this seven year treaty and defile the Temple.

Verses 16-20 state that the believing Jews will flee Jerusalem and Judah and go into the mountains to hide from the forces of the Antichrist. Revelation 12:6 is likely referring to this "*And the women (Israel) fled into the wilderness, where she hath a place prepared of God, that they should feed her there a thousand two hundred and threescore days*". Not only would Petra likely be the "*wilderness*" referred to but the time that they are there is three and half years, which is the second half of the Tribulation.

Verse 21 speaks of "*Great Tribulation*", which since it starts the second half of the seven years, lines up with the outpouring of God's great wrath spoken of in Revelation 16:1 "*And I heard a great voice out of the Temple saying to the seven angels, Go your ways and pour out the vials of the wrath of God upon the earth*".

The Return of Christ in Matthew 24

Verse 27 refers to cataclysmic events in the sky as it says "*lighting cometh out of the east*" and verse 29 says "*shall the sun be darkened and the moon shall not give her light and the stars fall from heaven and the power of the heavens shall be shaken*". This not only lines up with the end of the Tribulation period's judgments, where it is dark and the moon turns to blood but refers to all the universe preparing for the return of Christ.

Verse 28 has to be referring to the battle of Armageddon. Verse 28 says "*For wheresoever the carcase is, there will the eagles be gathered together*". This can be compared with Revelation 19:17 "*And I saw an angel standing in the sun; and he cried with a loud voice, saying to the fowls that fly in the midst of heaven, Come and gather yourselves together unto the supper of the great God*".

And verse 30 reads "*And then shall appear the sign of the Son of man in heaven and then shall all the tribes of the earth mourn, and they shall see the Son of man coming in the clouds of heaven with power and great glory*". This coincides with Revelation 19:11 "*And I saw heaven opened and behold a while horse, and He that sat upon Him was called Faithful and True…*".

Revelation goes into more detail about the battle of Armageddon but Matthew 24 gives other details, such as that the Lord will send His angels to not only bring all the godly to finally meet their Savior but destroy the wicked as well along with a great list of things that set all things right.[133]

The Lord's return establishes Jerusalem as a righteous city, has the Millennial Temple rebuilt, sees the nations judged, the righteous rewarded, fulfills all the promises that God made to the house of Israel, and establishes His servants from the New Testament era as under-rulers upon the earth "*And hast made us unto our God kings and priests and we shall reign on the earth*" (Revelation 5:10).

On this last point, that Christ brings with Him the New Testament Saints, let's dwell for just a moment. Imagine the pure splendidness of actually being with Christ, being without sin in His presence, and watching all things being fulfilled just as those who have believed the Bible have longed to see.

---

[133]. McClain, 501.

Chapter 20
The Nations Judged

Matthew 25:31-32 states *"When the Son of man shall come into his glory and all the holy angels with him, then shall he sit upon the throne of this glory: And before Him shall be gathered all nations: and He shall separate them one from another, as a shepherd divideth his sheep from the goats"*.

This judgment takes place at the end of the seven year Tribulation, which is seven years later after the rapture and this judgment takes place immediately after the battle of Armageddon. After the Lord's overwhelming victory, his first order of business is to eliminate the heathen and those that opposed Him from entering the Millennium.[134] Now this is not Christ gathering the unsaved for the Great White Throne judgment but only removing them from the population of the earth to hold them in Hades until that final day of judgment.

Dr. C.I. Scofield in his reference Bible says "This judgment is to be distinguished from the Great White Throne judgment Here there is no resurrection; the persons judged are living nations; no books are opened; three classes are present, sheep, goats, and brethren; the time is at the return of Christ; and the scene is on the earth. All these particulars are in contrast with Revelation 20:11-15.".[135] For in Revelation, the persons judged are said to be dead *"…and the dead were judged…"* (Revelation 29:12 and they are brought from hell *"…and death and hell delivered up the dead which were in them…"* (Revelation 20:13).

In Matthew 25, the terms "sheep" and "goats" are used, both long term representatives of different types of people, of course "sheep" being easily identified with those who listen to Christ and goats those who try to fit in but do not belong to the shepherd.

In verse 33, the Lord easily identifies them and separates them for the Bible says that not only do the sheep hear His voice but that he knows them. And though the goats may claim to

---

[134]. Spence and Exell, 480–481.

[135]. C.I. Scofield, *The New Scofield Reference Bible* (New York: Oxford University Press, 1967), 1037.

belong to Christ, Matthew 7 states that many shall claim to know Him but He will tell them that He never knew them.

To the sheep the Lord says "*Come ye blessed of my Father, inherit the kingdom prepared for you from the foundation of the world*" (Matthew 25:34). And to the goats or the unsaved He says "*Depart from me, ye cursed, into everlasting fire, prepared for the devil and his angels*" (Matthew 25:41).

The judgment of the nations will be a dark day indeed for the all the unsaved on the face of the earth. The prophet Zephaniah says "*Therefore wait ye upon me, saith the Lord, until the day that I rise up to the prey: for my determination is to gather the nations that I may assemble the kingdoms, to pour upon them mine indignation, even all my fierce anger for all the earth shall be devoured with the fire of my jealousy*" (Zephaniah 3:8).

God will judge the nations, sending the saved into the "*joy of the Lord*" and the unsaved into damnation.

Illustration of Jesus separating the saved from the unsaved, called in Matthew 24, the separating of the sheep from the goats.

Chapter 21
The Great White Throne

Nothing speaks of judgment like hearing the phrase "The Great White Throne Judgment". After the Millennium is over, all those who have died in their sins will be brought before the Lord at what Revelation 20 calls a "*Great White Throne*". This chapter will look at a few specifics and then answer some questions about who will be judged and how readers know when this will take place.

This Judgment Throne Is Great

We at first see that this throne and thus the judgment is called "*Great*", setting it apart from all the thrones of earth and all the thrones that have come before it. That it is white speaks to its absolute purity and holiness and righteousness in judgment and that no one who stands before it can claim injustice. Its greatness is also attested to by the statement "*from whose face the earth and heaven fled away and there was found no place for them*" (Revelation 20:11). Here this statement speaks to the fact that there can be no arguments against its judgment, no counsel or laws that might supersede it and no one can or ever will dispute its rulings. For as Dwight Pentecost says, it is the final ruling.[136]

Where Will This Take Place?

As to where the judgment takes place, it is interesting that it does not take place on earth or for that matter in heaven either, for as the above verse read, both earth and heaven could not stand before it. Pentecost says it takes place somewhere between the two, perhaps in the New Jerusalem that some think will be in the sky above the earth.

---

[136]. Pentecost, 423.

What Will Be Judged?

The judgment will be based on works.[137] Now at first that seems odd to those from an evangelical background as the Bible teaches that salvation is not based on works but purely and simply on God's grace. But that is just the point, they did not accept God's grace. The Baptist Commentary puts this well when it says concerning Revelation 20:13 "Each individual, one and all, according to or based on their works; their degree of punishment in the lake of fire and brimstone is fixed at the Great White Throne judgment, based on the manner and number of their wicked works…".[138]

You see, because they did not accept God's grace, they will be judged on the only thing they have, their actually lives. Notice in the passage in Revelation 20, that the "books were opened", showing that all men's deeds, words, thoughts, motives are recorded. But when we are saved, Christ's blood is applied to our records and we can then be found just in Him.

What Is Their Sentence?

And what is their sentence? Everyone there without exception, will be cast into the Lake of Fire "*And death and hell were cast into the lake of fire. This is the second death. And whosoever was not found written in the book of life was cast into the lake of fire*" (Revelation 20:14-15).

Who Will Be Judged at the Great White Throne?

Those that are judged are called dead "*And I saw the dead small and great, stand before God…*" (Revelation 20:12). But this is not for all those that have tasted death, but for those who have not been resurrected into life, but these are those who from all eternity past died in their sins and are now finally brought before the judge. So though there have been resurrections, it has been for first those who died in Christ, then those who were

---

[137]. Stanton, 260.

[138]. Garner, *Revelation*, 346.

living in Christ and lastly those who died looking for to Christ, being the Old Testament saints. So these before the Great White Throne are even not physically resurrected, but just brought before God. They are in a sense the only ones left after all the resurrections.[139]

Where Do The Judged Come From?

As to where they came from, it seems the passage covers all the options "And the sea gave up the dead which were in it and death and hell delivered up the dead which were in them (Revelation 20:13). But this verse is not giving different destination options but making clear that there will be no excuse for them not to stand trial. Physical location will not prohibit someone from appearing at the judgment

Some might say that if a body was buried at sea, that the body would of course, be destroyed at sea and never be seen again, but Revelation 20 says that regardless of whether a body has lasted, that that person will still be brought forth to stand at the Great White Throne Judgment.

If God can resurrect the saved who were lost at sea, burnt in a fire or turned to dust in the ground, then He can gather those souls from wherever they are kept to come to judgment.

Already Suffering in Hell Will Not Prohibit Someone from Appearing at the Judgment

Hell is not a prison but only a holding jailhouse, holding the accused until trial. No criminal gets to ignore a trial because he has already been incarcerated. And even in the United States' justice system today, if the defendant is found guilty, his time in jail is considered for his time, but since the sentence will be eternity, one's time in hell will not make a difference.[140]

---

[139]. Pentecost, 423-424.

[140]. Walvoord, 306–307.

Experiencing Death Will Not Prohibit Someone from Appearing at the Judgment

Some think that passing from this life of sin and disobedience to God places them outside the reach of judgment but it in fact does the opposite. It was in this life that they had every opportunity to repent and accept God's salvation. And when death came, instead of moving them past the point of God's punishment, it brought them into it.

When Will the Great White Throne Judgment Take Place?

On this, there is actually much agreement, as it seems that it can only take place at the end of the age.[141] As readers work through Revelation 19-20 and take note of events, the "Great White Throne" judgment is pushed further and further to the end of recorded time until it presses up against the beginning of eternity.

We first see that the Battle of Armageddon has taken place in the last part of chapter 19 and that satan is bound and confined to the bottomless pit in chapter 20, while the Millennium passes by "*And cast him into the bottomless pit and shut him up and set a seal upon him that he should deceive the nations no more, till the thousand years should be fulfilled…*" (Revelation 20:3).

Second, the "*Great White Throne Judgment*" is pushed further by the middle part of chapter 20, when satan is released to deceive those born during the Millennium "*And when the thousand years are expired, satan shall be loosed out of his prison and shall go out to deceive the nations…*" (Revelation20:7-8).

Third, it is pushed to the end when God sends fire from heaven and destroys satan and all those that followed him "*And they went up on the breadeth of the earth and compassed the camp of the saints about and the beloved city and fire came down from heaven and devoured them*" (Revelation 20:9).

---

[141]. Pentecost, 423.

And lastly, the devil is cast into the Lake of Fire once and for all, ending his time of tempting man and leading nations astray *"And the devil that deceived them was cast into the lake of fire and brimstone, where the beast and the false prophet are and shall be tormented day and night for ever and ever"* (Revelation 20:10).

And so with the Tribulation over, the Battle of Armageddon over, the Millennium over, satan once and for all vanquished and cast into the Lake of Fire, *"forever and ever"*, there is simply no where to put the *"Great White Throne Judgment"* other than at the end of time, the end of everything, where after it is eternity forever. The Baptist Commentary says of this "endless time and duration, without cessation, forever".[142]

Who Will Judge at the Great White Throne Judgment?

We are at first left with this question as the passage only says *"And I saw a Great White Throne and Him that sat on it…"* (Revelation 20:11). And the only other reference to God is in the next verse where they are but *"standing before God"*. So is this God the Father or God the Son?

Perhaps one can figure this out by considering a few things and comparing some Scripture. One can first consider that Christ is clearly the judge at the Bema Seat of Christ, which is where Christians are judged and rewarded. That Christ is the judge there is clear *"But why does thou judge thy brother? or why does thou set at nought they brother? for we shall all stand before the judgment seat of Christ"* (Romans 14:10).

And it seems clear that Christ will be the rewarder, which in a way is still a judge, at the end of the age for the believers *"And behold I come quickly and my reward is with me, to give every man according as his work shall be"* (Revelation 22:12). And so if Christ is the judge at the beginning of the end times at the Judgment Seat of Christ and if Christ is the judge at the end of the age, then it should not seem out of place for Him to be the judge at the Great White Throne judgment.

---

[142]. Garner, *Revelation*, 343.

But this writer realizes that there is no mention of Jesus in this passage and only a reference to *"God"* which brings to mind God the Father. But listen to what Jesus said of Himself for it seems that Jesus says that God has turned over all judgment to Him and that would make judgment seem fair. Though God of course has the right to judge man, as He is the Creator, but some of those being judged might claim that God the Father was never a man and did not live a life here on earth. But if Jesus is the judge, than what can man say, for Christ endured all temptations known to man and yet lived a holy life. So let's compare the passage in Revelation 20 and what Jesus spoke of Himself in John 5.

John 5		Revelation 20	
vs 25	"…the Son of God…"	vs 11	"…and Him that sat on it…"
vs 25	"The hour is coming…"	vs 11	"And I saw…"
vs 25	"…when the dead…"	vs 12	"And I saw the dead…"
vs 27	"And hath give him authority…"	vs 11	"…from whose face the earth and the heaven fled away…"
vs 27	"…to execute judgment…"	vs 13	"…and they were judged…"
vs 28	"…all that are in the graves…"	vs 13	"…and death and hell delivered up the dead…"
vs 29	"…and they that have done evil…"	vs 13	"…according to their works"
vs 29	"…of damnation"	vs 15	"And whosoever was not found written in the book of life was cast into the lake of fire"

Chapter 22
Conclusion

Prophecy can be challenging to the beginner. The many topics, from the Rapture to the Great White Throne Judgment, and the many prophetic passages, from the Ezekiel passage on Gog and Magog to the Dragon in the book of Revelation, can at first seem daunting and overwhelming, to not only understand but may seem difficult or even impossible to place in any chronological order. But as shown, when the faithful student of prophecy respectfully and carefully approaches this most interesting field, the Bible gives amazing fruit for the labor.

In the first several chapters, it was important to lay out some ground work, cover some bases, and build the foundation for correct interpretations. Seemingly, most of the mistakes that were brought up as examples of wrong interpretation, were from those who jumped to conclusions and wanted to get to what they thought was the interesting parts without the diligent study and work required to draw conclusions from complicated eschatological passages. And then being ignorant of major prophetic doctrines such as God's promise to the descendants of Abraham and how God's attention will turn again to Israel during the seven years of the Tribulation, can throw off any attempted understanding of passages in Revelation such as the Dragon and the Woman, as the interpreter will attempt to make them somehow symbolize the church, instead of Israel in the last days.

In the rest of the chapters, example after example was given to show how one prophetic passage can be used to help interpret another prophetic passage. Whether it is a fuller understanding of the crowns that will one day be offered to the saints at the Judgment seat of Christ or whether the Antichrist of the book of 1 John is the same as the Beast of the book of Revelation, comparing the passages of the Bible on these topics can not only shed light and a deeper and fuller understanding of each passage but can most often answer the question.

Even concerning the much arguable chronological timeline of end time events, there are passages in the Bible that provide small but meaningful pieces of the puzzle and may if nothing else, position some event before or after another event, and when all these pieces are looked at, studied and compared with a prophetic eye, they help place the major events in a likely order.

Proof text preaching, where one only looks at one prophetic passage alone, not only undercuts the ability to know the actual meaning of a text, but will likely cause the reader to misinterpret the text and will even more likely cause the reader to place that text incorrectly in the end time chronological timeline. As pointed out earlier, an example of this could be the erroneous view that those left behind in Matthew 24 are those that missed the Rapture, when they are in fact, those who had believed on Christ and were about to enter the Millennial kingdom.

Scripture explains Scripture and anyone who desires to understand prophecy should dig in for *"All scripture is given by inspiration of God, and is profitable for doctrine, for reproof, for correction, for instruction in righteousness: that the man of God may be perfect, thoroughly furnished unto all good works"* (2 Timothy 3:16-17).

And lastly, the Scriptures are so clearly inspired and proven by God Himself, that anyone who takes the time to look at them will be humbled by what God has said and what He has done and will come to believe that what He says will happen will happen. My prayer is that you, my friend, will believe in the great God of the Bible, the Great Savior of the cross and His coming, and that you will call out to be saved before it is too late.

One day, there will be but two groups standing before the Lord in heaven. One will be the saved about to enter into eternity in glory and the other will be standing before the Great White Throne of Judgment. Please I beg of you, make sure you are one of His servants, flawed but saved, imperfect but redeemed, perhaps even with questions but a believer!

Appendix
A Possible Timeline of Prophetic Events

Prophetic Event	When	Main Biblical Text
The Last Days	End of Church Age	2 Peter 2
Last Days Signs	End of Church Age	2 Timothy 3
Last Days Church	End of Church Age	Revelation 3
Rapture	End of Church Age	1 Thessalonians 4
Judgment Seat	Start of Tribulation	2 Corinthians 5
God's Wrath Begins	Start of Tribulation	Revelation 5
Tribulation Begins	Start of Tribulation	Daniel 9-12
Antichrist Revealed	Early Tribulation	2 Thessalonians 2
Antichrist Treaty	Early Tribulation	Daniel 9-12
Temple Built	Early Tribulation	Revelation 11
The Four Horsemen	Early Tribulation	Revelation 6
Tribulation Martyrs	Early Tribulation	Revelation 6-7
The 144,000	Early Tribulation	Revelation 7
The Seventh Seal	Mid Tribulation	Revelation 8
Demons Released	Mid Tribulation	Revelation 9
Gog and Magog	Mid Tribulation	Ezekiel 38-39
Israel turns to Christ	Mid Tribulation	Revelation 1

Abomination of Desolation	Mid Tribulation	Matthew 24
God's Angels Go To War	Mid Tribulation	Revelation 10
Two Witnesses Slain	Mid Tribulation	Revelation 11
Ark of Covenant In Heaven	Late Tribulation	Revelation 11
Satan Cast out of Heaven	Late Tribulation	Revelation 12
Unholy Trinity	Late Tribulation	Revelation 13
The Mark of the Beast	Late Tribulation	Revelation 13
Babylon Rebuilt	Late Tribulation	Revelation 14
God's Great Wrath	Late Tribulation	Revelation 15
Vials of God's Wrath	Late Tribulation	Revelation 16
Kings of the East March	Late Tribulation	Revelation 16
False Prophet/Harlot Church	Late Tribulation	Revelation 17
Destruction of World Church	Late Tribulation	Revelation 17
Babylon and Economy Falls	Late Tribulation	Revelation 18
Christ Returns to Earth	End of Tribulation	Revelation 19
Battle of Armageddon	End of Tribulation	Revelation 19
Christ Judges the Nations	End of Tribulation	Matthew 25
Millennial Kingdom Begins	Start of Millennium	Revelation 20
Millennial Kingdom	Millennium	Isaiah 2-11
Satan Released/Defeated	End of Millennium	Revelation 20

White Throne Judgment	End of Millennium	Revelation 20
Eternity Begins	Eternity	Rev. 21-22

Bibliography

"Arnold Murray: The Shepherd's Chapel." Let Us Reason Ministries. http://www.letusreason.org/poptea4.htm (accessed December 1, 2017).

"The Battle of Ezekiel 38-39: Part 2." Grace thru Faith. https://gracethrufaith.com/end-times-prophecy/the-battle-of-ezekiel-38-39-part-2/ (accessed December 21, 2017).

Benware, Paul N. *Understanding End Times Prophecy: A Comprehensive Approach.* Rev. ed. Chicago: Moody, 2006.

Carson, D. A., Douglas J. Moo, and Leon Morris. *Introduction to the New Testament.* Grand Rapids: Zondervan, 1994.

Chafer, Lewis Sperry. *The Kingdom in History and Prophecy.* Chicago: Bible Institute Colportage Association, 1936.

———. *Systematic Theology.* Vol. 5. Grand Rapids: Kregel, 1976.

Champlin, Edward. *Nero.* Cambridge, Massachusetts: Harvard University Press, 2003.

"The Church in Prophetic Perspective." Grace to You. https://www.gty.org/library/study-guides/40-5115/the-church-in-prophetic-perspective (accessed March 10, 2016).

Cottrell, Leonard. *The Lost Pharoahs.* New York: Columbia University Press, 2005.

Garner, Albert. *General Epistles.* Baptist Commentary. Lakeland, FL: Blessed Hope Foundation, 1985.

———. *Revelation.* Baptist Commentary. Lakeland, FL: Blessed Hope Foundation, 1985.

Goetsch, John. *Contemporary Compromise: Standing for Truth in an Age of Deception*. Lancaster, CA: Striving Together, 2010.

Graham, Billy. "Do You Think the Antichrist Is Already Alive? Or Is the Antichrist Just a Symbol or a Figure of Speech?" Billy Graham Evangelistic Association. https://billygraham.org/answer/do-you-think-the-antichrist-is-already-alive-or-is-the-antichrist-just-a-symbol-or-a-figure-of-speech/ (accessed October 7, 2017).

Green, Jay P., ed. *The Interlinear Bible*. Lafeyette, IN: Sovereign Grace, 1985.

Howard, Kevin, and Marvin Rosenthal. *The Feasts of the Lord: God's Prophetic Calendar from Calvary to the Kingdom*. Nashville: Thomas Nelson, 1997.

Ice, Thomas, Randall Price, and John F. Walvoord. *Ready to Rebuild: The Imminent Plan to Rebuild the Last Days Temple*. Eugene, OR: Harvest House, 1992.

Jones, Nathan. "Will the Antichrist Be Killed and Resurrected?" The Christ in Prophecy Journal. http://christinprophecyblog.org/2009/06/will-antichrist-be-killed-and/ (accessed October 12, 2017).

Joosten, Jan. "Textual Criticism and the Septuagint." http://ohb.berkeley.edu/Joosten,%20LXX%20in%20OHB.pdf (accessed December 21, 2017).

Josephus, Flavius. "The Antiquities of the Jews." Documenta Catholica Omnia. http://www.documentacatholicaomnia.eu/03d/0037-0103,_Flavius_Josephus,_The_Antiquities_Of_The_Jews,_EN.pdf (accessed October 30, 2017).

———. *Josephus: Thrones of Blood*. Edited by Toni Sortor. Uhrichsville, OH: Barbour, 1988.

Kearley, Furman. *The Conditional Nature of Prophecy.* Montgomery, AL: Apologetics Press, n.d.

LaHaye, Tim. *Revelation: Illustrated and Made Plain.* Grand Rapids: Zondervan, 1974.

———, ed. *Prophecy Study Bible: King James Version.* Chattanooga, TN: AMG, 2000.

LaHaye, Tim, and Thomas Ice. *Charting the End Times: A Visual Guide to Understanding Bible Prophecy.* Eugene, OR: Harvest House, 2001.

———, eds. *The End Times Controversy: The Second Coming Under Attack.* Eugene, OR: Harvest House, 2003.

Lewis, C.S. *Mere Christianity.* San Francisco: Harper, 2009.

Martin, Walter. *The Kingdom of the Cults.* Rev. ed. Edited by Ravi Zacharias. Minneapolis: Bethany House, 2003.

Matson, Daniel. "The Great Sign of Revelation 12 Occurs in 2017." Signs of the End. http://watchfortheday.org/1260tetrad.html (accessed September 29th, 2017).

McCallum, Dennis, and Gary DeLashmutt. "Double Reference in Biblical Prophecy." Xenos Christian Fellowship. https://www.xenos.org/essays/double-reference-biblical-prophecy (accessed February 23, 2016).

McClain, Alva. *The Greatness of the Kingdom: An Inductive Study of the Kingdom of God.* Winona Lake, IN: BMH Books, 2001.

Miller, Stephen M. *Stephen M. Miller's Illustrated Bible Dictionary.* Uhrichsville, OH: Barbour, 2013.

Mounce, Robert. *The Book of Revelation.* The New International Commentary on the New Testament. Grand Rapids: William Eerdmans, 1977.

Newman, Randy. "What Do You Say to Your Jewish Friends about Jesus?" C. S. Lewis Institute. http://www.cslewisinstitute.org/What_Do_You_Say_to_Your_Jewish_Friends_about_Jesus_page1 (accessed December 21, 2017).

Pentecost, J. Dwight. *Things to Come: A Study in Biblical Eschatology.* Findlay, OH: Dunham, 1958.

Phillips, John. *Exploring 1 and 2 Thessalonians.* John Phillips Commentary Series. Grand Rapids: Kregel, 2001.

———. *Exploring Revelation.* John Phillips Commentary Series. Grand Rapids: Kregel, 2001.

———. *Exploring the Book of Daniel.* John Phillips Commentary Series. Grand Rapids: Kregel, 2001.

———. *Exploring the Gospel of Matthew.* John Phillips Commentary Series. Grand Rapids: Kregel, 2001.

Pinelli, Richard. "The Kingdom of God: The Best News You Could Hear!" Life, Hope & Truth. https://lifehopeandtruth.com/prophecy/kingdom-of-god/ (accessed November 28, 2017).

Pink, Arthur W. *The Antichrist.* Blacksburg, VA: Wilder, 2008.

Piper, John. *Counted Righteous in Christ? Should We Abandon the Imputation of Christ's Righteousness?* Wheaton: Crossway, 2002.

Price, James D. "Rosh: An Ancient Land Known to Ezekiel." *Grace Theological Journal* 6, no. 1 (1985): 67–89.

Price, Randall. *Jerusalem in Prophecy.* Eugene, OR: Harvest House, 1998.

———. *The Coming Last Days Temple.* Eugene, OR: Harvest House, 1999.

Reagan, David R. "Will the Antichrist Be a Jew?" Bible Prophecy Blog. http://www.bibleprophecyblog.com/2009/05/will-antichrist-be-jew.html (accessed October 10, 2017).

"The Red Heifer: The Original Ashes." The Jewish Temple Institute. https://www.templeinstitute.org/red_heifer/original_ashes.htm (accessed April 23, 2016).

Rhodes, Ron. *Northern Storm Rising: Russia, Iran, and the Emerging End-Times Military Coalition Against Israel.* Eugene, OR: Harvest House, 1995.

Richardson, Joel. *Mideast Beast: The Scriptural Case for an Islamic Antichrist.* Washington, D.C.: WND Books, 2012.

Rochford, James. "The Regathering of Israel." Evidence Unseen. http://www.evidenceunseen.com/articles/prophecy/the-regathering-of-israel/ (Accessed April 11, 2016).

Ryrie, Charles. *Ryrie Study Bible.* Chicago: Moody Press, 1994.

Scofield, C. I., ed. *The New Scofield Reference Bible.* New York: Oxford University Press, 1967.

Slick, Matt. "What Does the Shepherd's Chapel Teach?" https://carm.org/what-does-shepherds-chapel-teach (accessed March 18, 2016).

Spence, H.D.M., and Joseph S. Exell. *Pulpit Commentary.* 23 vols. Peabody, MA: Hendrickson, 2011.

Sproul, R. C., Jr. "Harold Camping: False Prophet?" Ligonier Ministries. https://www.ligonier.org/blog/harold-camping-false-prophet/ (accessed December 1, 2017).

Stanton, Gerald B. *Kept from the Hour.* Miami Springs, FL: Schoettle, 1991.

Thompson, J. A. *The Bible and Archaeology*. Grand Rapids: Eerdmans, 1962.

Torres, Alan. "Jack Van Impe: Bible Prophecy Teacher Extraordinaire or Confused Prophet?" The Biblicist. http://biblicist.chrisapproved.com/bible/vanimpe.html (accessed November 30, 2017).

Tozer, A. W. *Preparing for Jesus' Return: Daily Live the Blessed Hope*. Minneapolis: Bethany House, 2012.

Walvoord, John F. *The Revelation of Jesus Christ.* Chicago: Moody, 1989.

Westminster Confession of Faith. Glasgow, Scotland: Free Presbyterian Publications, 1958.

Whedon, Daniel. *Daniel Whedon's Commentary on the Old Testament.* Vol. 8. N.p.: GraceWorks Multimedia, 2012.

"Where Are the Ten Lost Tribes of Israel?" https://www.geni.com/projects/Where-are-The-Ten-Lost-Tribes-of-Israel/3474 (accessed October 20, 2017).

About the author

    Randy grew up on a farm near Solsberry, Indiana with his brother Rob and sister Rhonda. His parents Jim and Cindy faithfully took him to church each and every week and he accepted Christ as a boy in Sunday school at Grace Baptist Temple, a church in the nearby city of Bloomington, a church to which he is still so very thankful for to this day.

After serving in the army in the armored cavalry, teaching history and starting and running a business, he was called into ministry at the age of 35.

After selling his home and business, he went back to school to Baptist Bible Graduate School of Theology in Springfield, Missouri, where he received a Masters in Church Ministry while learning about practical ministry from the many Baptist Bible Fellowship churches in the area.

Afterwards, he and his wife Deanna and their children, James and Victoria moved to Ames Iowa to start a church in 2003. They rented a little building for services while remodeling an old barn to be their first church building. And in the more than fifteen years pastoring there, Randy has led the church in three more building projects and Heartland Baptist is a thriving, growing, soul-winning, giving church today.

While in Iowa, Randy earned another Master's degree in religious studies from Faith Baptist Seminary and eventually received his Phd in Theology from Louisiana Baptist University, focusing on Eschatology.

Randy is very involved in the Iowa Baptist Fellowship, and tries to encourage and be a blessing not only to the many pastors there but to missionaries that pass through the state as well.

He still pastors in Ames, loves winning people to Christ and teaching the Bible. He is thankful to the Lord for calling him into the ministry and thankful to his wonderful wife Deanna, his children, James and Tori and daughter-in-law, Kayley and his congregation who have encouraged him all along the way.